What's in a Name?

What happens when you are living in the small Hamlet of Anytown, USA and, on your way to get the mail one day, you notice that your local newspaper has hung out its shingle and taken occupancy of the building next door to you?

Well, if you've been harboring a hidden passion for writing all hell may be ready to break loose. How do we know this? Because we've lived it.

Every once in a while you go down a rabbit hole that really catches your fancy. There's actually an interesting twist to this analogy; the bait that led us down this rabbit hole was Rabbit Hash.

In working on an article about dogs, we came across this small Kentucky town which, in addition to the notoriety it gained from rabbit eating, felt that the country hillbilly image they were seeking could only be enhanced by adopting the tradition of electing a dog for mayor.

We subsequently spent the next three years researching the most bizarrely named places on the planet and employing our irreverent approach to stylize our stories.

What you are holding in your hands here are the fruits to those efforts. How 'bout we name you as our "Reader of the Year" and let the name games begin?

What's in a Name?

Your Geography Hall of Fame

by

Tim & Deb Smith

Pandamensional Solutions, Inc.

Mendon, New York

This book contains both original and previously published work. Some material contained herein represents the opinions of the individuals quoted and not necessarily the opinion of the authors. In some cases, for metaphorical purposes, this work contains fiction. In such circumstances, names, characters, places and incidents are either the product of the authors' imagination or are used fictitiously. Any resemblance to actual events or locales or persons, living or dead, is entirely coincidental.

Limit of Liability/Disclaimer of Warranty: While the publisher and the authors have used their best efforts in preparing this book, they make no representations or warranties with respect to the accuracy or completeness of the contents of this book and specifically disclaim any implied warranties or merchantability or fitness for any particular purpose. No warranty may be created or extended by sales representatives or written sales materials. Neither the publisher nor author shall be liable for any loss of profit or any other commercial damages, including but not limited to special, incidental, consequential or other damages.

COPYRIGHT © 2021 BY TIM & DEB SMITH

Published by Pandamensional Solutions, Inc., Mendon, NY

Cover artwork by Emma Rizzella-Roberts

Back cover photos by Scott and Savanna Smith

Cover design by Catarina Carosa

ALL RIGHTS RESERVED

INCLUDING THE RIGHT OF REPRODUCTION

IN WHOLE OR IN PART IN ANY FORM

ISBN-10: 1-938465-12-1
ISBN-13: 978-1-938465-12-3

What others are saying about Tim & Deb Smith's

What's in a Name?

I've read all of the Smiths' books and am more entertained with every page I turn. I'm captivated by their irreverent style and no-holds-barred approach to tackling their subject matter. They take no prisoners.

~ Microsoft Accounts Manager Keith Partington

As a real estate agent, dealing with geographical places is basically my job and this was the most wonderful trip around the world that I've ever taken. Furthermore, the whole thing went down without ever having to leave the comfort of my reading room. I got to sail all five oceans and travel all seven continents. I visited scores of places I'd never been before and came away enriched by the experience.

~ Entrepreneur Katherine M. Gonyea

In trying to describe the Smith writing style two things rise to the surface as being the descriptors which most characterize their work. They write non-fiction, but I often find myself thinking, "This is better than anything you could makeup." The other thing I love about their style is that they write in such a way that it makes you feel like they're right in the room talking to you.

~ Historian Mike McGory

I've never really considered myself a history or geography buff but merely looking at the Table of Contents had me totally intrigued. How can there actually be real places with such obscene (in some cases literally) and quirky names. The storytelling is superb. I can honestly say this was the most fun I ever had with geography.

~ Dr. Frederick J. Marra

"Greetings from Christmas Island and it's lovely to hear from you! I have just read your book and it is fantastic. So much thought and attention to detail, certainly one of my favourite CI pieces of writing."
~ Christmas Island Tourism Director Jahna Luke

Dedication

*We are who we are because of
where we were when*

Table of Contents

CHAPTER 1 ~ STORYLINE SAMPLER
1~Storyline Sampler

CHAPTER 2 ~ FOOD FOR THOUGHT
10~Eggs and Bacon Bay, Tasmania, Australia
12~The Bottle, Alabama
13~Oatmeal, Texas
14~Two Egg, Florida
15~Burnt Corn, Alabama
16~The Big Apple~ New York City
17~Cookietown, Oklahoma

CHAPTER 3 ~ DRINKS ARE ON US
19~Once Brewed, Northumberton, England
19~Twice Brewed, Northumberton, England
20~Smut Eye, Alabama
20~Whiskeytown, California
20~Toad Suck, Arkansas
21~Beer, Devon, England
22~Beer Bottle Crossing, Idaho

CHAPTER 4 ~ HIGH TIMES
23~Weed, California
24~Zigzag, Oregon
24~Skyhigh, California
24~Stoner, Colorado
26~Knockemstiff, Ohio

CHAPTER 5 ~ HOW DO YOU LIKE THOSE MELONS?
29~Sugar Tit, South Carolina
30~The Office Girls, Antarctica
30~Titty Hill, West Sussex, England
31~Lake Titicaca, Peru/Bolivia
33~Nipple Peak, Antarctica

CHAPTER 6 ~ COCK-A-DOODLE-DOO
34~Condom, France
35~Blue Ball, Pennsylvania
35~Kick in de Kök, Estonia
35~New Erection, Virginia
36~Wetwang, Yorkshire, England

CHAPTER 7 ~ WHAT'S UP, PUSSYCAT?
37~Beaverlick, Kentucky
38~Big Beaver, Saskatchewan, Canada
39~Pussy, France
39~Pussy Creek, New Zealand
40~Bimbo, Central African Republic
40~Muff, Ireland
41~Vagina, Russia
42~Twatt, Scotland

CHAPTER 8 ~ THE JOY OF SEX
44~Come By Chance, Newfoundland, Canada
44~Dildo, Newfoundland, Canada
46~Blow Me Down, Newfoundland, Canada
47~Orgy, France
47~Phuket, Thailand

47~Hooker, Oklahoma
48~Climax, Colorado
49~Intercourse, Pennsylvania
50~Kissing, Bavaria, Germany
50~Humptulips, Washington
51~Pennycomequick, Devon, England
51~Oral, South Dakota
52~Tightsqueeze, Virginia
52~Spread Eagle, Wisconsin
53~Horneytown, North Carolina
54~Sexmoan, Philippines
54~Fucking, Austria
57~Virgin, Utah
58~Virginville, Pennsylvania

CHAPTER 9 ~ WORDPLAY
59~Key West, Virginia
59~Key, West Virginia
60~Zzyzx, California
60~Truth or Consequences, New Mexico
61~Lake Chargoggagoggmanchauggagoggchaubunagunamaugg, Massachusetts
62~Llanfairpwllgwyngyllgogerychwyrndrobwllllantysiliogogogoch, Wales
63~Taumatawhakatangihangakoauauotamateaturipukakapikimaungahoronukupokaiwhenuakitanatahu, New Zealand

CHAPTER 10 ~ EXCLAMATIONS!
 – QUESTIONS?
 – COMMANDS.
64~Saint-Louis-du-Ha!-Ha!, Quebec, Canada
65~Eek, Alaska
65~Good Grief, Idaho
66~Who'd Thought It, Texas
66~Why, Arizona
66~Whynot, North Carolina
67~Pity Me, Durham, England
68~Rest and Be Thankful Mountain, Scotland

CHAPTER 11 ~ IT'S A NUMBERS GAME
69~Thirteen Martyrs, Philippines
70~Eighty Four, Pennsylvania
70~Eighty Eight, Kentucky
74~Ninety Six, South Carolina
75~Wonowon, British Columbia, Canada

CHAPTER 12 ~ NOT FOR NOTHING
78~No Name, Colorado
79~No Place, Durham, England
79~Nowhere, Oklahoma
80~Point No Point, Washington

CHAPTER 13 ~ DON'T BE SO NEGATIVE
81~Taylor's Mistake, New Zealand
82~Very Stupid, France
83~Idiotville, Oregon
83~Tightwad, Missouri
84~Useless Loop, Australia
84~Misery Bay, Michigan
85~Peculiar, Missouri
85~Little Hope, Texas
86~Disappointment Islands, French Polynesia
87~ Dumb Woman's Lane, Sussex, England

CHAPTER 14 ~ FROM BORING TO BLAND
88~Boring, Oregon
89~Dull, Perthshire, Scotland
90~Bland, New South Wales, Australia
90~Lost, Aberdineshire, Scotland
91~Okay, Oklahoma
91~Uncertain, Texas

CHAPTER 15 ~ OUR BODY OF WORK
92~My Large Intestine, Texas
93~Big Arm, Montana
93~Port Circumcision, Antarctica
93~Scrath Ankle, Alabama
94~Leg-In-Boot, Vancouver, British Columbia, Canada

CHAPTER 16 ~ PAIN IN THE ASS
96~Backside, Aberdeenshire, Scotland
96~Scratchy Bottom, Dorset, England
97~Six Mile Bottom, Cambridge, England
97~Bit Butt Mountain, North Carolina
97~Kiester, Minnesota
98~Anus, France
98~Scratch My Arse Rock, Cook Islands
99~Ragged Ass Road, Northwest Territories, Canada
101~Superior Bottom, West Virginia

CHAPTER 17 ~ OOH, THAT'S GROSS!
102~Booger Hole, West Virginia
103~Brokenwind, Aberdeenshire, Scotland
103~Middelfart, Denmark
104~Pee Pee, Ohio
104~Poo Poo, Hawaii
105~Shitterton, Dorset, England
106~Shit, Iran

CHAPTER 18 ~ BATMAN: THE DARK KNIGHT
107~Bat Cave, North Carolina
108~Gotham, Wisconsin
108~Joker Mine, Arizona
109~Alfred, New York
109~Penguin, Tazmania, Australia
110~Batman, Turkey

CHAPTER 19 ~ A ZOOTOPIAN EXPERIENCE
113~Monkey's Eyebrow, Kentucky
114~Rabbit Hash, Kentucky
117~Worms, Germany
117~Chicken, Alaska
123~Mousie, Kentucky
123~Bird-in-Hand, Pennsylvania

CHAPTER 20 ~ JUSTIFYING THE JIM THORPE THEFT
125~Jim Thorpe, Pennsylvania

CHAPTER 21 ~ HOME FOR THE HOLIDAYS
128~Santa Claus, Indiana
130~North Pole, New York
130~Santa Claus, Georgia

131~Christmas, Florida
132~North Pole, Alaska
134~Santa Claus Arizona
138~Christmas Island, Australia
140~Christmas Pie, Normandy, England

CHAPTER 22 ~ THE WILD WILD WEST
141~Tombstone, Arizona
142~Death Valley, California
143~Rough and Ready, California

CHAPTER 23 ~ YOU'RE KILLING US
145~Kill Devil Hills, North Carolina
146~Deadhorse, Alaska
148~Slaughter Beach, Delaware
149~Dead Horse Bay, New York
150~Fresh Kills, New York
151~Deadwood, South Dakota

CHAPTER 24 ~ GO TO HELL
153~Hell, Norway
154~Hell For Certain, Kentucky
154~Hotazel, South Africa
155~Satan's Kingdom, Massachusetts
155~Satan's Kingdom, Vermont
156~Satan's Kingdom, Connecticut
157~Hell, Michigan

162~Addendum #1 – The Top 25

173~Addendum #2 – The Poetry

Foreword

By Educator Beth Thomas

"What's in a name? that which we call a rose by any other name would smell as sweet…" is a line from Shakespeare's *Romeo and Juliet* that author, Tim Smith must have explained at least two hundred times in his three decades as an English teacher in a suburban high school. Those years of entertaining and educating sophomoric teenagers have resulted in this raucous, well-written, often hilarious compilation of short stories about places with intriguing names. Deb and Tim have spent years researching these special places and have created a unique book full of facts, fun, mayhem, and even the macabre.

That naughty limericks often accompany the anecdotes might not surprise readers as they peruse chapters about body parts, profanity, and sex, but It's all a FUN romp in the hay from Virgin, Utah to Intercourse, Pennsylvania and around the world. You'll remember Lake Titicaca, Peru because "when you can combine boobs and poop in one lake, you might as well have fun with it." And you will never forget what happened to the body of one of the most famous American athletes. Readers will learn that it all really DIDN'T happen at the O.K. Corral but you can travel to Okay, OK.

Masters of double entendre, authors Deb and Tim Smith, make readers of a certain age giggle as they read word play with seminal references to pop culture and literary canon. Did you know that a country filed suit over the name Batman? Just place your copy of the book in a place where you can read it every day and you will want to read and re-read your favorite snippets. Be rewarded with an enticing, dare I say titillating, travel itinerary of adventures well-researched and referenced for your irreverent perusal.

Laugh, enjoy, educate your friends, garner your next "cocktail" party joke, applaud the brazen audacity of the Austrian widow whose town limit sign provides outrageous entertainment in her front yard. Make the book a gift for a witty friend or make it a glove compartment staple for traffic jams and Covid-19 waiting lines.

Acknowledgements

This whole thing got started one morning when we simply went out to get the mail. We live in the downtown section of a small town in Upstate New York with a population of about a thousand. The office of our local newspaper happens to be right next door to us and we love to tell stories. That can be a dangerous combination.

On the morning in question, we crossed paths with the newspaper publisher and shared our rather unique personal back story. That prompted the response that, "You should share that story in the paper." A week later we hit the presses for the first time and the essence of that story can be enjoyed in the "About the Authors" segment in the back of this book.

Soon thereafter we had taken over the back page for a weekly "Sentinel Lifestyles" feature called "Life With the (Word)Smiths." In general, our feature covers an eclectic variety of topics including entertainment, sports, travel, history and human interest. "We're all over the place" is a comment that ironically can be applied to both our writing for the paper and the theme of this book which you are about to read.

So, our writing has expanded to the point we are currently composing three columns a week for the paper and this is our third book we've published. In a variation of a basketball statistic often heard, rather than scoring a triple-double, we have notched a double-triple. And we have had some fun along the way!

After launching our newspaper career, our publisher Chris Carosa, began encouraging us to write a book. The stars, for us, aligned in the beginning of 2019 when we connected the dots on some historical events and came to realize that occurring within a 30-day period that coming summer would be the 50th anniversaries of First Man on the Moon,

Chappaquiddick, the Manson Murders, Woodstock and one other thing… it also happened to be the 50th anniversary of the day we met.

We were waiting for a sign from God and this seemed to be thrust down upon us like a lightning bolt hurled here from Heaven. We needed to pick one of those 50th anniversary events, take it by its literary horns and run with it. That led to the composition of our first book, *The Beatles, The Bible & Manson: Reflecting Back with 50 Years of Perspective*.

So what to do for a follow up? The answer that just kind of fell into our laps was a thematic compilation of all the material we had generated for the paper which we titled, *Tit For Tat Exchanges ~ Tim & Deb's Greatest Hits*. The first half of the title is a reference to the single line we wrote that generated the greatest response from our readers.

At one point we did a story on Easter Island which is a territory of Chile located off the western coast of South America in the Pacific Ocean. One part of our Easter Island coverage featured a dispute between the territory of Easter Island and its mother country of Chile which was described as a tit-for-tat exchange.

We love to analyze and play with words and that storyline gave us pause to ponder… isn't "tit-for-tat" such an interesting little colloquialism? Does not that pause to ponder give one cause to wonder, "What exactly is tat? How do I get some? And where can I turn it in for the other thing?"

In *What's in a Name? ~ Your Geography Hall of Fame* we have tried to combine our love for historical geography and penchant for storytelling. We spent a few years researching this project and the components of this book basically had to satisfy two criteria. To even achieve consideration the place needed a unique name, but in order to make this book it also needed to be accompanied by a story worthy of sharing and one that lent itself to our irreverent writing style.

We hope you appreciate our efforts on this one and as this third book comes out we are actually finishing up the writing on our fourth. Here's a preview. It's tentatively titled *Listing Dangerously to the Left* and everything in the book is written in the form of some kind of list. In terms of subject matter it's reminiscent of our second book *Tit For Tat Exchanges* in that it spans an eclectic collection of topics.

So at this point please allow us to become your tour guides for a serendipitous sojourn. We are about to take you on an educational and entertaining trip around the world. How 'bout we buckle up and hit the road!?

Tim & Deb Smith
Mendon, New York
April 1, 2021

Chapter 1
STORYLINE SAMPLER

We have literally searched every corner of the globe to entertain and educate you on this one. We'll go from the frozen heights of the **North Pole** to the sweltering depths of **Death Valley**. We'll visit with Santa and Satan. And if you've read our previous books, rest assured that irreverent devil-may-care attitude we exude will be on full display. We'll take you to heaven and hell to prove it.

What we have assembled for you here is a collection of the most unusual and intriguing place names on the planet and the fruits of a few years of labor coming up with the most clever and creative ways to tell their stories. The motif we will employ for the rest of this chapter is that we will **bold** and capitalize everything that is an actual place which is included in our book. We'll start out by getting you high and we'll gently bring you back down.

HIGHS & LOWS - For example in our "High Times" marijuana chapter we take a very calculated approach to the mind-altering experience. We begin by having you score your reefer in **Weed**, California. Then we head up the coast to **Zigzag**, Oregon for the rolling papers. After rolling a fat one and blazing up, it's off to **Skyhigh**, California. Then of course, our ultimate destination will be **Stoner**, Colorado for the Annual Colorado Invitational Bong-a-Thon.

But of course, what goes up must come down. Be careful or you could find yourself dumped on **Dumb Women's Lane**, and left with **Little Hope** in **Idiotville**. Or you could be stranded at **Misery Bay** in the **Disappointment Islands** reliving the **Useless Loop** of **Taylor's Mistake**.

If all of this calamity drives you to drink, we've got you covered. In our alcohol chapter, "Drinks Are on Us," we'll head down to **Whiskeytown**, find out how **Beer Bottle Crossing** got its name, and perhaps even more curiously, how does the town of **Toad Suck** have a name that's based upon the consumption of alcohol? The answer to that one will leave you feeling a little green.

Our "All of God's Creatures" chapter has our single most favorite segment in the book, but we'll share a few other critters before we get to our fave. We'll ponder the question of whether a **Bird-in-Hand** is worth a **Monkey's Eyebrow** or, for that matter, if monkeys even have eyebrows. We'll supply the details and let you decide if you'd rather eat **Rabbit Hash** or a Diet of **Worms**.

Here's a teaser regarding Rabbit Hash. Since 1998, this town in Kentucky has elected a dog to the office of mayor. Their first female mayor was Lucy Lou who certainly lived up to the promise she campaigned upon when she declared herself, "The Bitch you can count on!" To bring you completely up to date, Lucy Lou was succeeded by current Mayor Brynneth Pawltro.

But best of all, we're going to head up north to **Chicken**, Alaska. Nobody on the planet has embraced their quirky name to the point this place has. Their website is hilarious and perhaps most titillating of all, they have a panty cannon. We're sure you'll want to experience the delicious details of that one!

> *No plumbing, don't be panic-stricken*
> *But your pace to the outhouse might quicken*
> *You're pissed off and swearing*
> *But at least you're bearing*
> *Gifts saying, "I got laid in **Chicken**!"*

We've always been huge bat-fans ever since the campy 1960's Adam West TV series. So when we stumbled across the fact that there's a place in North Carolina called **Bat Cave**, we could not resist the urge to flesh out that concept for a complete chapter. The results were rousing.

We traveled to **Gotham** to confront the **Penguin** at **Joker Mine**. Appropriately, however, the most intriguing storyline emerged from **Batman** itself. There's a town in Turkey that bears that name and has taken on a somewhat bizarre relationship with the Dark Knight. We'll tell you about how they've done all of the following:

- Sued Warner Bros. over the movies.
- Blamed Batman for an increased teen suicide rate.
- Attempted to gerrymander their boundary into the shape of the Bat-Signal.

WORD PLAY - If you'd like to get excited, confused or bossed around, we've got a chapter for you called "Exclamations! Questions? and Commands." We'll cover Charlie Brown's signature exclamation of **Good Grief!** and we will address the classic philosophical questions of **Why** and **Why Not**? And when it's all said and done you will be directed to **Rest and Be Thankful**.

We have one chapter where "It's a Numbers Game." If you think the scoop on **Eighty Four** is good, wait until you get the lowdown on **Eighty Eight**. And what happens when the good citizens of one Canadian town form a committee to come up with a name for their community and decide to hold a meeting at the local tavern? We'll also sojourn to the South Pacific to visit **Thirteen Martyrs** in the Philippines and return to America to play ball and hear the story behind the first Major League Baseball player to wear a number higher than 50.

Don't be **Uncertain**; our chapter called "From **Boring** to **Bland**" is more than just **Okay**. We will tell you the true story of how three towns in three different countries banded together in a unique "League of Extraordinary Places." Rather than being despondent over their uninspired town names, the communities of **Boring**, Oregon; **Dull**, Scotland; and **Bland**, Australia have bonded together in a "Trinity of Tedium" and managed to turn all three communities into tourist destinations, a concept that isn't very Boring at all.

In our "Ooh, That's Gross" chapter you'll find out that there really is a town in West Virginia named **Booger Hole**. Confronting our fear of flatulence, we will visit both **Middelfart** and **Brokenwind**. Our sophomoric antics will include **Pee Pee** and **Poo Poo**. And you know what? If you don't like it, we don't give a **Shit**, or a **Shitterton** for that matter.

OUR BODY OF WORK – We hope you like "Our Body of Work" here. We're going to have you covered inside and out on this one. We'll delve to the core and get the story on **My Large Intestine** which can be found in Texas and to take care of that itch, we'll head east to Alabama where you can **Scratch Ankle**.

We'll find out why in the world a place would come to be known as **Port Circumcision**, but we're going to save the real kicker for last. How do you think **Leg-In-Boot** got its name? We'll save the details for later, but it all starts when a severed leg wearing a boot washed up on the shore in a Canadian town.

It washed up on the shore over there
*Just one **leg in** a **boot** solitaire*
What the hell do we do?
We just feel inclined to
Stick the leg on a stake in the square

Our "Pain in the Ass" chapter is actually not all that painful, with lots of potential for segues. How better to deal with a **Scratchy Bottom** than to **Scratch My Arse**? We have a **Backside** story or two that don't sound very attractive. Would you rather your date hail from **Six Mile Bottom** or **Big Butt Mountain**? It's a **Ragged Ass Road** to either of those places. But we promise to leave you on a very positive note. We will close the chapter with the arousing story of a truly **Superior Bottom**.

THE JOY OF SEX – Be advised that we will provide gender equity in our analysis of the human body. After the literal covering of our collective asses, in the following chapters of the book we'll do due diligence to the honoring and recognition of both male and female body parts. Just like we all did in high school, why don't we start at the top and work our way down.

We think you'll love our chapter saluting one of God's most beautiful creations, the female breasts. Call them what you want – you could go with one of the more common euphemisms such as hooters or melons, or you can go with something exotic like brown-eyed Susans or the dynamic duo. Rack them up any way you prefer, we will honor them in that forthcoming chapter.

In our drive for gender equality we're going to move on over to the males for our "Cock-a-Doodle-Doo" chapter. For all you guys out there, be prepared for the fact that the news here is going to range from "that feels so good" to "that hurts like hell."

On the upside, we will be giving you a **Wet Wang** and on the downside you'll feel what it's like to get a **Kick In de Kök**. You may be able to avoid the good and the bad by simply wearing a **Condom**. That's another story in and of itself.

PUSSYFOOTING AROUND ~ Giving equal time to the ladies we'll move on to our "What's Up, Pussycat!" chapter, which will be an adventurous one. You will find out what it's like to be in New Zealand, caught up **Pussy Creek** without a paddle. Then we'll head back to the U.S. for the ultimate fantasy where you'll find out what it's like to complete one **Beaverlick** only to discover it's time to immediately move on to the **Big Beaver**. Next it's off to the U.K. where we'll take you from the land of **Muff** to the town of **Twatt**.

If Scotland wasn't already your favorite country, it will be soon. Believe it or not, the Scots have two Twatts. Yep, there are only two geographic locations on the planet called "Twatt" and they're both in Scotland. Here Kitty, Kitty.

Our chapter on sex called "The Joy of Sex" will certainly be the best fucking chapter in the book. It's actually in Austria; **Fucking**, that is. It's a true town with a titillating tale. How should you determine if you'd like to continue with this chapter? Please allow our next sentence of wordplay to become your litmus test regarding your continuance. Keep reading if...

You'd like to see a **Spread Eagle - Virgin - Come By Chance** in **Horneytown**; it might be a **Tightsqueeze** but **Blow Me Down** that **Bimbo** will **Sexmoan** before her **Climax** during **Intercourse**. There's also the part where you get to put the **Dildo** in the **Vagina** of the **Hooker** while she's performing **Oral**. And after that deed is done you can relax, kick back, and watch your favorite episode of *The Big Bang Theory*, **Pennycomequick**.

LANGUAGE BARRIERS ~ One conceptual thread that runs through this book is this scenario where centuries ago people in a foreign country gave their town a name that had a funky meaning in English which had no connection whatsoever to any meaning in the native language. In the 9th century A.D. when a community of Austrians named their town Fucking, who knew? But a millennium later with the internet linking a global community, everyone knows.

So what are the modern-day ramifications for foreign towns whose names have racy meanings in English? There are basically two, one fairly innocent and one problematic. The one that is no big deal for the most part is people posing for pictures, although some people have been known to pose by the Fucking sign in positions designed to add a depth of realism to the photo op.

What is the bigger problem for these towns whose names have funky meanings in English? Their signs become targets for theft which incurs the cost of replacement. This facet of the issue must be balanced out with the reality that the photo ops actually generate genuine economic benefits for the community.

We'll admit it, if we were on that once in a lifetime European vacation, and the realization that we were less than an hour away from Fucking put us in the mood, we'd know that we have two options. We could stay at the hotel and do it, or we could drive to the town and do the photo op.

FUCKING OPTIONS - Assume we're given the options of making love at the hotel or making the trip to Fucking to get a picture. Let's face it, of these two options one we could do when we get back to the states. If we want to get our picture taken at the only official Fucking sign in the world, we'd have to drive there for the photo op and once we're there, we'd probably stop for lunch and a few drinks. So that's how the racy name actually generates real revenue for the town.

And after dinner how can you not head to the local souvenir shop? The Fucking shot glasses are guaranteed conversation starters for the adults. And what kid would not be thrilled to open up their gift Christmas morning and find out that Santa has left them an item of clothing embellished with the phrase, "My parents went to Fucking and all I got was this lousy t-shirt."

So what have most of these foreign places with the funky names done? In Fucking, they have voted three times about whether or not to change the name and the bottom line is that Fucking is still Fucking. The French towns of **Anus** and **Pussy** remain Anus and Pussy. The only exception of note to this trend has been that Sexmoan in the Philippines did change its name to save its signs.

Of course this is an issue which can play out in both directions. The town of Kolkhoz in Russia decided to change its name in 1991. What did they opt for? The Russians in Kolkhoz decided to change their name to Vagina. As we know, if you can secure the signs there is money to be made on tourism. What frisky young Russian couple could resist an invite for a Valentine's voyage into Vagina?

HAPPY HOLIDAYS ~ For some people on the planet the song "There's No Place Like Home For the Holidays" takes on a whole different meaning. Their Christmas themed monikers make them merry 365 days a year.

In an escalating layer of holiday hilarity we'll share with you the stories of one **Christmas**, two **North Pole**s, and three **Santa Claus**es, all in the United States. After that we'll fly across the pond to England for dessert. What's on the menu there? How about a nice big slice of **Christmas Pie**?

On the rooftop sometimes Santa pauses
Naming places with holiday causes
*Our one "**Christmas**" extols*
*There are two "**North Pole**s"*
*And then alas three "**Santa Claus**es"*

The story of Christmas, Arizona is one that really got to us for reasons we look forward to sharing. That town was started from scratch in 1937 by a zany lady named Nina Talbot. She billed herself as the biggest real estate agent in California, which might have come off as just egotistical were it not for the fact her weight of 300 pounds certainly added an air of duplicity to the claim.

Once one of the premiere attractions on Route 66, today it's a ghost town. The rise and fall of Christmas, Arizona is a roller coaster story with some tantalizing twists and turns, and perhaps an inevitable ending. Today the rattlesnakes outnumber the reindeer. Oh, but there was a day!

THE OLD WEST ~ While we're on the subject of rattlesnakes we might as well plug our "Wild Wild West" chapter. You better be **Rough and Ready** because this one's a real shoot 'em up. We will share with you the stories of how **Death Valley** got its name and what really happened during the shootout at the O.K. Corral. We'll muddle some myths that have prevailed as most people's go-to take on what happened at the most famous gun fight in the history of the Old West.

We'll let you in on the secret that Wyatt Earp was not the leader of the good guys and oh, by the way, the gunfight did not occur at the O.K. Corral. It's just that "The Shootout at C. S. Fly's Photo Studio" doesn't have quite the same ring now, does it?

DEATH AND HELL ~ Next, we've got bad news and more bad news. How bad can it get? At the end of this book you're going to die in one chapter and in the following chapter you're going to go to **Hell**. But don't worry, we're going to go with you.

Before we put you on that hellbound train, however, let's cover the prerequisite. In our chapter called "Till Death Do Us Part," our journey will take you from **Deadhorse**, Alaska to **Dead Horse Bay**, New York. We can then wax poetic and check out all the **Fresh Kills** at **Kill Devil Hills**.

After we've killed you off, we're going to finish the job and send you to **Hell**. Because you know how much we love to take care of you, we're awarding you the following bonus. We are actually going to take you to Hell twice. There's one in Michigan and one in Norway. No extra charge.

What will it be like when we get there? Not surprisingly it's going to be **Hotazel**, which can be found in South Africa. There are only two place names that come up three times in our book. The first is Santa Claus and the second is **Satan's Kingdom** which can be found in the states of Connecticut, Massachusetts and Vermont.

Here's a little bit of irony for you; did you ever realize that Satan and Santa are anagrams? Well, the fact that we spend time thinking about things like that is probably the reason that we're going to **Hell For Certain,** which is in Kentucky.

PETA PEOPLE ~ At this point we will have the People for the Ethical Treatment of Animals choreograph our segue from Chapter 1 to Chapter 2. We want to make it clear that we are amongst the greatest animal lovers on the planet, but we do occasionally butt horns with PETA.

The organization makes exactly two appearances in the book and they're a little over the top in each one. Ironically one PETA appearance is in the "Till Death Do Us Part" chapter which we introduced a few paragraphs ago and the other is the very first component of the next chapter.

In both situations PETA approaches towns and asks those communities to change their names which the organization believes to be contrary to its goals and purposes. The general concept that any town would want to change a long established historical name because it may have some vaguely offensive animal implication is sketchy from the get-go and PETA goes 0-2 in their endeavors.

In Chapter 21 we'll tell the story of why PETA wanted **Slaughter Beach**, Delaware to change its name and we won't keep you waiting for long for the second reference. Our lead story in Chapter 2 is the PETA sojourn to **Eggs and Bacon Bay**, Tasmania.

Chapter 2
Food for Thought

Everybody loves to eat so that seemed like a logical launching point for this fabulous foray into food. This chapter will touch upon some appetizing entries such as **Cookietown**, and others like **Burnt Corn** which doesn't sound quite as mouthwatering. We'll have a chance to hit the bottle at **The Bottle** and we'll even fill you in on why New York City is referred to as the **Big Apple**. But first let's head to the land down under and get the frying pan sizzling.

EGGS AND BACON BAY, TASMANIA

It was a beautiful sunny-side-up morning in Eggs and Bacon Bay, Tasmania, when suddenly the mood was pooh-poohed by those prissy PETA people pandering political correctness, or the purported lack thereof, on the part of the residents of Eggs and Bacon Bay. PETA was proffering the proposal that E&BB change its name to a more animal-friendly "Apple and Cherry Bay."

Prior to filing their petition for the change in 2016, PETA Australia's associate director of campaigns, Ashley Fruno, had submitted a letter to Mayor Peter Coad of Eggs and Bacon Bay informing him that Tasmania had the highest level of lap band surgery in all of Australia, and to help halt that hideous health statistic, Fruno suggested that residents abstain from cholesterol and fat-laden bacon and eggs.

She went on to advocate a dietary diversion toward the fresh plant produce grown locally in Tasmania's Huon Valley as that would be "just what the doctor ordered." In an interview Fruno added that the change to apples and cherries from eggs and bacon would "... promote not only the local economy, but also healthy eating and kindness to animals. Considering the high levels of cholesterol and saturated fat in both eggs and bacon," she continued, "your area may as well be called 'Heart Attack Bay,'" subtlety clearly not being a PETA strong suit.

For the record, there was a basis, albeit sketchy, for the PETA proposal. The Huon Valley in which Eggs and Bacon Bay is located, is famous for its fruit orchards, with apple and cherry trees proliferating the valley. But just because there is a method to the madness, doesn't mean it's not madness.

FIGHTING BACK WITH FLOWERS ~ Not that they needed to defend themselves, but the egg-eaters of Eggs and Bacon Bay were quick to point out to PETA that, truth be told, the historic name to their town had nothing to do with chickens or pigs. Tasmania's E&BB is named after a regional wildflower commonly known as eggs and bacon, whose petals are a mixture of the sunny yellow of egg yolks and the deep red of bacon.

But the town was open minded and agreed to put the topic up for a vote. Eggs and Bacon Bay had a population of 102 at the time and the vote on the name change was rejected by a tally of 100-0. Two people were out of town. "The idea was ludicrous," Mayor Coad said, adding, "I feel pretty strongly about it. This is our heritage; it is our history."

We like Egg-Bacon Bay to defeat a
Name changing vote to complete a
Move to just place
The egg on the face
Of those tree-hugging vegans at PETA

So the story of Eggs and Bacon Bay ends with whipped cream and a cherry on top. What the hell, we'll even throw on an apple slice if it would make PETA happy. Here's our one takeaway. If you ever consider having lap band surgery, just remember, PETA is watching.

THE BOTTLE, ALABAMA

Imagine it's 100 years ago, you're driving through rural Alabama, and up ahead you notice a bright orange 64-foot high wooden soda bottle looming on the horizon. What do you do? Well, let's face it, if it were 100 years ago and you were driving through rural Alabama in the first place, it's probably a pretty safe assumption that life has not dumped you in the lap of luxury.

You have not traveled the world and you haven't seen it all. So what do you do when you happen upon literally the biggest bottle in the world? You bet your homespun country ass you're going to stop and check it out.

Hell, bigger names than yours have been lured in. The honor roll of visitors to The Bottle ranges from the sublime to the sophisticated. Grand Ole Opry singer Minnie Pearl stopped by to set a spell and President Franklin D. Roosevelt once ascended the second floor balcony to deliver a speech.

The Bottle is located sixty miles northeast of Montgomery near Auburn University. The original bottle was built in 1924 by John F. Williams, owner of the Nehi Bottling Company, with the intention of garnering a bit of roadside publicity. In addition to that purpose, it also contained a grocery store and a service station in the bottom, and became a popular meeting spot.

SIZE OF THE BOTTLE ~ Here are the complete stats on the bottle's physical description. In addition to standing 64 feet tall, the wooden structure measured 49 feet in diameter at the base, and 16 feet in diameter at the cap. Above the service station area, which was outside of the bottle, was a balcony deck that was used as a gathering spot and party area. Above the ground floor grocery store, the second and third floors were living quarters and storage respectively. There was a spiral oak stairway running through the neck of the bottle which had windows enabling it to be used as an observation tower. The bottle cap served as the roof.

Unfortunately the reign of the bottle would last for but a scant dozen years. The Bottle lost its bottle when it burned down in 1936. The visual of that event must have been spectacular with the giant orange bottle engulfed in giant orange flames.

> *In 'Bama they love fun and games*
> *Some places down there have great names*
> *But their Bottle of Nehi*
> *That stood sixty feet high*
> *Went up in a blaze of orange flames*

Although the structure no longer exists, a historic plaque and a photograph mark the location, and Alabama maps still list the area as "The Bottle."

OATMEAL, TEXAS

Fifty-six miles northwest of Austin is the rural Texas community of Oatmeal, which was originally founded by German settlers. Despite the fact that the population has dwindled to 20 people, there has been some good news as of late. The big event of the year is the annual Oatmeal Festival, held over the Labor Day weekend, which attracts an international crowd of hundreds.

There are two competing theories on the etymology of the town's name and they seem equally viable to us. Here they are.

Theory #1 ~ The primary commercial entity in the early era of the town were the oat mills which were constructed here. This theory advocates the premise that "oat mill" morphed into "Oatmeal" as a name for the town.

Theory #2 ~ The area's first mill owner was one Fritz Othneil. Along the same lines as the previous theory, this possibility suggests that "Othneil" morphed into "Oatmeal."

Located on a significant state crossroads, at one point Oatmeal was a fairly hoppin' hamlet. But that ended in 1950 when new interstate highways took Oatmeal off the beaten path. By the late '70's the population had dwindled to around twenty farming families and, horror of horrors, Oatmeal was no longer on the menu – it had been removed from the official Texas state map.

That fact initiated a call to arms. Oatmealers, disheartened by being dissed, answered with an admirably ambitious plan. They banded together with nearby Bertram to create the concept of an "Oatmeal Festival."

Looking for a sponsor, organizers contacted every major national producer of oatmeal. Only one responded, but one turned out to be all they needed. National Oats climbed on board and the Oatmeal Festival was born.

LET'S GET FESTIVE ~ The festival has been held on Labor Day Weekend every year since 1979. During the celebration, this tiny town attracts the aforementioned international crowd. Oatmeal tasting options are so vast they could extend even the smile of the William Penn caricature on the front of the Quaker Oats cylinder-shaped box. Our favorite from last year's listings was white chocolate raspberry symphony.

And we'll finish with the best news of all. While the town will never again be a major state crossroad, it's back on the map! Because of the festival's newfound notoriety, the official state map of Texas once again includes Oatmeal.

TWO EGG, FLORIDA

Here's our Two Egg teaser on this town lying in the eastern part of the Florida panhandle with a population of about 3,500. In a Two Egg takeoff, using the speech device employed by the legendary *Batman* villain Egghead, Vincent Price might have worded it as follows. "Two Egg is an egg-stremely egg-citing town with an Egg-squisitely Egg-straordinary story." Two Egg was also the childhood home of Academy Award winning actress Faye Dunaway and a legendary monster, a "mini-Bigfoot" called the Two Egg Stump Jumper! There are many claims to fame in Two Egg.

Let's start with the name. There was one general store in town and during the Great Depression poor families would often bring in eggs from their farms and barter for goods. That general premise led to one specific story. As the tale goes, a traveling salesman was at the store one day when some children were sent in by their mother. All they had for payment was a pair of eggs, causing the store owner to complain that he was living in "nothing but a two-egg town."

When the salesman later needed to send a package of goods to the grocery, he simply addressed it to "the two-egg store." The name stuck, the post office eventually adopted it, the Florida Department of Transportation added the name to the map, and it's been Two Egg ever since.

TWO EGG TALKS – At this point, we will defer to the Two Egg officials with whom we spoke and proffered the request for them to put together a brief description of the town in their own words. The one-sided review of the Two Egg town reads like this:

"Yes, Two Egg is a real place. Located amidst the farms, woods and lakes of Jackson County, Florida, we have no city government, no city taxes, no city services and no city attitudes! Two Egg is a place where people still wave as they pass, neighbors know and care about their neighbors and life is lived with a touch of Southern charm and hospitality."

Poached, scrambled or sunny-side up, we found ourselves egg-cited to egg-splore. That being said, we will be wary of the aforementioned Two Egg Stump Jumper who is known to roam the woods and swamps between Two Egg and Lake Seminole.

The Stump Jumper is an upright beast, the sightings of which have the creature only half the height of your typical Big Foot or Sasquatch and lighter in color. Standing about four feet tall, the Stump Jumper's white fur is accentuated by the long trail of gray hair streaming behind his head as he runs.

He is usually seen at night running across dirt roads through the headlights of oncoming cars. Reverting to the Egghead motif, we employed earlier, please allow us to make the following egg-splicit egg-sclamation. If he dares cross our path, we will egg-spertly egg-spand egg-scrutiating efforts to egg-sterminate him. Egg-cellent!

BURNT CORN, ALABAMA

Today Burnt Corn appears frozen in time like a movie set. We'll get to that story in a moment, but first let's tackle the topic of the town's name. There are a few competing legends about how Burnt Corn achieved its moniker. Some say European settlers burned the Indians' corn fields and others say Indians burned the settlers' corn. Either way, conflict between the two groups climaxed at the Battle of Burnt Corn in 1813, which the Native Americans won.

Here's the "frozen-in-time" story about modern-day Burnt Corn. While it is still a viable community with a population of around 300, the four buildings that occupy each of the town's four corners are all empty and preserved as an historical museum showcasing early 20th century rural Alabama architecture. When you visit Burnt Corn today, you can take photos of four historical landmarks which include Lowrey's general store & post office, the doctor's office and two churches.

Before he died, town patriarch J.F.B. Lowrey, who already owned one of the four buildings, bought the other three, closed everything permanently, and established a trust to maintain the four corners of Burnt Corn in perpetuity as a museum and historic site.

If you plan to visit Burnt Corn for the historic photo op, we have a tantalizing twofer with which to tempt you. Just 12 miles down the road lies Monroeville, Alabama, a small town which is able to make a legendary literary boast. It happened to be the home town of both Truman Capote (*In Cold Blood*) and Harper Lee (*To Kill a Mockingbird*). The two future authors were childhood friends there in the 1930's and the museum in Monroeville pays tribute to their accomplishments.

THE BIG APPLE ~ NEW YORK CITY

As the largest city in the United States, New York City has embraced a few different nicknames over the years. It's been called the "Empire City", the "City so Nice They Named It Twice," and the "City That Never Sleeps." However, the one nickname that seems to stand out among the rest is the "Big Apple." There aren't any apple orchards in New York City, so how did the city earn this particular nickname? Here's the story of how NYC became the "Big Apple."

FIRST MENTION ~ The earliest mention of New York City as the "Big Apple" came from a book published in 1909 titled *The Wayfarer in New York*. In the story, the author uses the metaphor of a giant fruit tree to describe the United States. New York was referred to as the "Big Apple" because it was the largest city in the country.

Although it was officially the first mention of the nickname, that book did not cause the nickname to stick. That wouldn't happen for another decade. In the 1920's the *New York Morning Telegraph* writer John J. Fitz Gerald began to refer to the city as "the big apple" in a series of horse racing articles, thus constituting the first continuing usage of the term.

THE JAZZMAN - It would be a musical reference rather than a literary one that would spread the phenomenon of the nickname throughout the country and around the world. In the 1920's, jazz was the musical rage and jazz had a jargon all its own.

When a musician got a gig, they would refer to this feat as an "apple." There were many apples on the road to success, but the most prestigious prize, the biggest apple, could only be plucked from the tree branches of the biggest city in the country.

So, hypothetical situation, Louie Armstrong and Duke Ellington are out for drinks in L.A. after both performing California concerts. In discussing their upcoming schedules Armstrong says, "Next month I'm playing the Apollo Theatre in Harlem." Ellington's response may well had been, "So you scored the Big Apple!"

COOKIETOWN, OKLAHOMA

This town owes its name to the gratitude of one young boy. The small crossroads community in southern Oklahoma had one general store in the early 1900's that was run by Marvin Cornelius who had a propensity for handing out cookies to children.

On one such occasion the grateful recipient thanked Cornelius exclaiming, "I'm never ever gonna leave this Cookietown!" The store owner thought the compliment was sweet and adopted it. Despite its yummy name, Cookietown is more of a ghost town today—just a few residents and a church.

Later on in the book we'll be doing Christmas and the combination will be cookies and milk. But let's get this party started on a high note, how about some cookies and booze? In the next chapter the drinks will be on us.

Chapter 3
DRINKS ARE ON US

Now that we've eaten, it's time for an after dinner drink. Let the party begin. In this chapter we'll span the gamut; how 'bout a beer with a whiskey chaser? And we will provide the answers to questions that have been pondered for generations. Why don't we head down to **Whiskeytown**, find out how **Beer Bottle Crossing** got its name, and perhaps even more curiously, how does the town of **Toad Suck** have a name that's based upon the consumption of alcohol? The answer to that one will leave you feeling a little green.

Underwater you see the town's crossing
Whiskeytown had us turning and tossing
Just try to rhyme Toadsuck
Nightmares… what the fuck!
Let's go get high at Beer Bottle Crossing

ONCE BREWED, ENGLAND & TWICE BREWED, ENGLAND
    These are actually two separate towns which are located right next to each other and share an intermingled storyline where, in the name game, one moniker plays off the other. As fate would have it, Twice Brewed was first named. Here's that story.
    TWICE BREWED – In 1751 a road was being built across this area in central England and the workers stopped into the local tavern to collectively quaff some pints of ale. Everyone complained that the ale wasn't strong enough and urged the innkeeper to "brew it again." The rest, as they say, is history with Twice Brewed becoming the name of first the inn, and then the town.
    ONCE BREWED – Now, sally forth almost two centuries to the neighboring town where a new youth hostel was being opened in 1934. The owner was a teetotaler named Lady Trevelyan, and during the hostel's dedication speech she observed that it was uncomfortably close to the Twice Brewed Inn. "We will serve nothing stronger than tea,"

she said. "I hope even that will only be once-brewed." And again, the rest is history.

Playing upon the uniqueness of their names, combined with their proximity, the twinned villages feature some signage that salutes their situation. There is a single billboard between the towns and travelers heading west on Military Road will be hailed by the greeting "Welcome to Once Brewed." Coming from the other direction drivers will see "Welcome to Twice Brewed" on the other side of the same sign.

SMUT EYE, ALABAMA

Smut Eye is a small community in southeast Alabama. While once a fairly bustling little hamlet, only the abandoned general store remains from its more vibrant era.

The name was derived from the fact that the men were inclined to hang out at the blacksmith's shop and drink moonshine around the fiery furnace. When they would eventually return home it was no secret to their wives where they had been. The men would be covered with smut from head to toe, except for their eyes.

WHISKEYTOWN, CALIFORNIA

Today, Whiskeytown rests at the bottom of a shot glass, so to speak. In 1962 Whiskeytown Creek was dammed to create Whiskeytown Lake. So what was once a bustling mining town in the 1800's was intentionally flooded to create a community of lakeside cottages.

Here's the somewhat eerie side note… on a sunny day when the water is calm, the current residents of Whiskeytown can see the buildings of the original Whiskeytown lining the floor of the lake.

TOAD SUCK, ARKANSAS

Located on the Arkansas River in the central part of the state is Toad Suck, Arkansas, current population zero. Oh, but there was a day! There are two competing theories as to the origin of the name. We'll do the worst first. As we have a little fun with rhyme there, let us clarify that statement by saying that Theory #1 is not weak in terms of credibility. The two theories are probably equally viable; Theory #2 is just a lot more fun.

Theory #1 - This scholarly approach bases the name upon the fact that the first Europeans to thoroughly explore the area were the French. It espouses the theory that Toad Suck is a corruption of a French phrase meaning "a narrow channel in the river."

Theory #2 - In the 19th century, steamboats actively traversed the Arkansas River. There was an inn and adjacent dock at the location that came to be known as Toad Suck which became a frequent watering hole for the captains and crews of the boats. While the boatmen would partake at the tavern, they would become so inebriated the locals described their behavior by saying, "They suck on the bottle until they swell up like toads." Hence, the name Toad Suck.

The tavern is long gone, but the legend and fun live on at Toad Suck Daze. This would be the town's annual summer festival which used to be held at Toad Suck Park but it got so big it had to be moved to the neighboring town of Conway. Kudos to the Toad Suckers for their clever pun in naming their festival where they are clearly defaulting to Theory #2. If you drink enough in Toad Suck you'll be in a daze for days.

BEER, ENGLAND

The beautiful picturesque village of Beer is a coastal town located in southwest England. Surrounded by white chalk cliffs, the rocky beach is lined with fishing boats still bringing in their daily catches, and Beer is blessed with some of the most breathtaking coastal walks in the country. Who knew there would be national rankings for such a thing as this, but the village was also recently named as the top picnic spot in the U.K. because of its stunning view of the beach and village from the hillside.

The stark cliffs of Beer are home to a unique type of bacteria, so unique in fact that in 2008, Beer bacteria microbes were sent to the International Space Station to see if they could survive. We're not sure exactly what this means, but after a 2-year experiment many of the Beer bacteria were still basking in the afterglow of outer space survival.

If you think being in Beer will undoubtedly give you the desire to down a few, there are plenty of places to partake of a pint. When legendary smuggler Jack Rattenbury dropped the anchor on his life of seafaring crime, he retired to Beer. It was there that ironically, with the help of a clergyman, Rattenbury wrote his memoirs quaffing brews on Beer Beach. No bull.

BEER BOTTLE CROSSING, IDAHO

This picturesque spot is located in a heavily forested area of Adams County which is located near Boise in the southwestern part of the state. The location is near a scenic view overlooking a lake and it is this natural beauty that indirectly led to the unique name. Because of the setting being both serene and secluded, it became a hangout spot for the local party people who were known to fire up a few joints (see next chapter) and throw back some cold frosty beverages by these crossroads.

When local clean-up crews would make the morning rounds, the smell of the weed would have wafted away, but unfortunately still remaining would be the empty bottles, the "carry in – carry out" directions being sometimes ignored. Hence the name. The population is actually zero because Beer Bottle Crossing is located in Payette National Forest and, as we found out when we called Adams County, it is not legal for civilians to reside in a national forest.

Chapter 4
HIGH TIMES

We're going to start this chapter with an organized step-by-step process to getting you high and we'll finish with a component where we'll throw virtually every drug in the book at you. We gave some serious thought to the sequencing of the components of this series. Obviously the first thing in your process is that you have to score your pot, so let's go to **Weed**, California and do just that.

With weed in hand you will next need some rolling papers, so let's roll on to **Zig Zag**, Oregon to pick those up. After rolling a fat one and blazing up, it's off to **Skyhigh**, California. Then of course, our ultimate destination will be **Stoner**, Colorado for the Annual Colorado Invitational Bong-a-Thon. If you'd like to have your name added to the mailing list, just let us know. We have connections.

In Weed she'll score pot from a donor
In Zigzag some papers they'll loan her
While tokin' she'll fly for
She'll soon be Skyhigh for
That Bong-a-Thon fired up in Stoner

WEED, CALIFORNIA

Weed is a town of almost 3,000 people located in northern California. Its name came from its founder Abner Weed who arrived in 1897 and launched a lumber business that is still the primary component of the town's economy.

The town's drug stores are thriving because there's a corps of cannabis-loving Californians who feel like if you get your medicinal marijuana in Weed it adds an air of authenticity to the entire experience. The town's motto is "Weed like to welcome you."

ZIGZAG, OREGON

Now that you've scored your weed, you'll be needing some rolling papers, so let's head off to Zigzag, a village located smack-dab in the middle of the Mt. Hood National Forest in north central Oregon. The name was first used by early explorers to describe the flow of the Zigzag River which, obviously, zigs and zags its way through the community. When a post office was established in 1917, the village needed an official name and they went straight to "Zigzag."

The Zigzag Inn was built in 1927 and in 1933 Camp Zigzag was constructed as Oregon's first Civilian Conservation Corps camp, which was charged with building trails and camps in the national forests of Oregon. In 1937 President Franklin Roosevelt even visited Zigzag to salute the environmental effort. But things have quieted down since then and the post office closed in 1974. There are no longer any commercial entities in Zigzag, but the Mt. Hood National Forest is still overseeing the government's forest management service there. Maintaining the legal level of levity we're looking to be the connecting thread of this chapter, now that we have our rolling papers, it's time to move into the lightning round of our game.

SKYHIGH, CALIFORNIA

The name is only a bit of an exaggeration; while it's not sky high, its way up there. At an elevation of 7,041 feet, this small community is well over a mile above sea level. It's located in Calaveras County, home of the "celebrated jumping frog" immortalized by Mark Twain in what was his first major literary success.

After celebrating our Skyhigh status, let's get stoked for stoner.

STONER, COLORADO

This town was established in 1888 in southwest Colorado. We could not find much information about the history of the town except for the fact that it did have a post office from 1917-1954. But by the end of the 20th century Stoner had become a ghost town with the only remaining hint of its history being nine empty buildings.

The word stoner of course took on a new meaning in the age of marijuana, but that would not seem to have any impact upon the ghost town. That all changed, however, in 2012 when Colorado passed its Amendment 64, legalizing marijuana.

That prompted one old hippie named Frank McDonald to buy the entire town, all nine dilapidated buildings, and appoint himself mayor of Stoner which had a population of two. In addition to himself McDonald said there was also "an old lady named Mary Jane who lives in a little hunter's shack up on Stoner Creek."

What was old McDonald's plan? The colorful entrepreneur bought the property with plans to turn it into a cannabis-friendly resort. Stoner's Facebook page identifies it as, "A premier cannabis tourist destination where the great outdoors meets mile-high cannabis." What the average observer may have considered a ramshackle assemblage, McDonald saw as a destination music venue: Mary Jane's Stoner RV Park, Grill & Bar and Events Center.

GREAT EXPECTATIONS ~ Mary Jane's website proclaimed that "numerous nationally known music acts would be playing during the spring-summer of 2012" but the "schedule expected by January 2012" is yet to materialize, so not a lot seems to be happening in the redevelopment of Stoner.

That being said, Stoner did appropriately become home of the 32nd Annual Colorado Invitational Bong-a-Thon which fired up in 2015. This gala advertised "competitive toking," and was expected to draw around 1,000 cannabis connoisseurs. The giant pot party in the quasi town raised reefer-madness fears in southwest Colorado.

The Bong-a-Thon obviously had to be an underground event during its earlier years but when marijuana was legalized in Colorado it was a whole new ball game. When organizers secured a Stoner location for the event that was on 52 private acres there wasn't a whole lot the protesters could do about it. While we don't have any reviews of the festivities, July 31–August 2, 2015 was designated to be a storied Stoner weekend, "a carnival of competitive cannabis consumption with contests, camping and music."

KNOCKEMSTIFF, OHIO

This is one of those quirky place names where multiple theories exist as to the etymology. We'll get to those eventually, but this is also one of those places where there's an overlying story that's so overwhelming, we really need to go with that first to put the later things into perspective.

There used to be a road sign, pocked with bullet holes, marking the beginning of this little village southwest of Chillicothe in southern Ohio, but someone stole it a few years ago, and there hasn't been much urgency about putting up another one. The residents already know where they are, and not many strangers pass through. One of the two main roads in town, Shady Glen, eventually runs out of pavement and turns to dirt.

Knockemstiff has a favorite son, so to speak, in the form of author Donald Ray Pollock and we became so caught up with this storyline to the point where we ended up reading his first two books.

Pollock grew up in this backwater town, along with many of his cousins, and he used the village as both the setting and the title for his first book, *Knockemstiff*, a collection of linked stories in which nearly all the characters are violent or abused, and most are serious drinkers. One party animal actually swigs Old Grand Dad from his car ashtray.

Drugs of choice include marijuana, meth, mescaline, hashish, angel dust and OxyContin. And the use of drugs in Knockemstiff was not only prolific, it was also creative. While sharing the suggestion that you not try this at home, who knew that Seconal could be inventively internalized in suppository form?

Knockemstiff provides an alternate universe to the American dream. Living here are dirt-poor residents mired in desperate trailer-park lives surviving on microwave TV dinners. Jobs are scarce. Sex is brutish and loveless. Fistfights erupt out of the smallest slights, serving as pathetic proof of a man's existence.

Drugs, not religion, offer the only solace – however fleeting. Bodybuilders inject steroids while nursing home aides steal prescriptions. While one Knockemstiffer scarfs up drugs intended for his girlfriend's stroke-victim father, another down-and-outer sniffs Bactine. As a commercial campaign began to tout in 1955, Children Really Like Bactine – It Doesn't Sting. While it may not have stung the kids who were spraying it in the '50's, it may well have been stringing out the adults who were snorting it in the '90's.

The Devil All the Time, Donald Pollock's second book, is also partly set here, and check out this excerpt from the prologue. "Four hundred or so people lived in Knockemstiff in 1957, nearly all of them connected by blood through one godforsaken calamity or another, be it lust or necessity or just plain ignorance."

These days the village is a lot tamer than it must have been back then, when people from elsewhere gave it a wide berth. The two bars that thrived during the decades of decadence, Hap's and the Bull Pen, have closed, and the cinderblock general store that Pollock's parents used to run has been remodeled into a house for one of his two sisters.

The ball field that a Vista volunteer built in the late 1960's is overgrown with weeds and briars, the base paths infield dirt discernible only upon the closest inspection. The outfield fence has fallen, home plate has found a new home and the pitcher's mound has been purloined.

Many of the original houses have been burned down or knocked down and replaced with double-wide mobile homes. This is the kind of situation which would seem to make a native want to break down and cry. But Pollock seems to just look at the entire clusterfuck and say, "It is what it is." The stark honesty with which Pollock tackles his subject matter is uniquely juxtaposed against his nonjudgmental detachment.

Let's move on now to the origins of the name Knockemstiff, Ohio and you'll notice an irony here. The tempestuous amoral antisocial antics that characterized the town in the 1960's through 1990's tales, told by Donald Ray Pollock in the books described above, are reflected in all three of the competing theories as to the origin of the name. There is no clear favorite.

Theory #1 - The Fighting Women Theory - This one says that in the 1800's, a traveling preacher entering town came across two women fighting over a man. The preacher doubted the man was worth the trouble and said that someone should "Knock 'im stiff."

Theory #2 ~ The Cheating Husband Theory ~ This tells the tale of a woman who confronted her preacher after a Sunday morning worship service, informing the clergyman that her husband was cheating on her. She wanted the preacher's advice, and his response was a straightforward "Knock 'im stiff."

Theory #3 ~ The Moonshine Theory ~ Yet another explanation is that the name is slang for the moonshine or homemade liquor that many of the locals manufactured. Residents say that moonshining was formerly common in the area surrounding the community, which had a reputation for rowdiness.

Yes, Virginia, there really is a town called Knockemstiff. Barely a crossroads southwest of Chillicothe, it's a little patch of hillbilly Appalachia in southern Ohio. But trust me, dear Virginia, you wouldn't want to live there.

Chapter 5
How Do You Like Those Melons?

We hope you caught a buzz with our marijuana chapter and if you're like us you may now be in the mood to move onto some sexual shenanigans. We do go to Kissing and cover 1st base later in Chapter 8, but this chapter is going to focus on 2nd base, figuratively speaking.

This is our salute to one of God's most beautiful creations, the female breasts. Call them what you want – you could go with one of the more common euphemisms such as hooters or melons or you can go with something more exotic like brown-eyed Susans or the dynamic duo. Rack them up any way you prefer, we are here to honor them in this chapter.

Sugar Tit is a name that's unique
The Office Girls flaunt their mystique
Titicaca just will
Adore Titty Hill
Antarctica has Nipple Peak

SUGAR TIT, SOUTH CAROLINA

Good news. This one is even sweeter than it sounds! We'll get to that in a minute, but first we'll fill you in on what's bouncing in Sugar Tit these days. The town is located near Spartanburg in the northwestern part of South Carolina.

Joe's Fishing Lake and Restaurant is going strong, the General Store is now an auction house and a good time can still be had at the Sugar Tit Racetrack. The most economy-stimulating fairly-recent news is that a BMW Performance Center was built in 2010 so the population in the area is actually increasing.

So, where did the name come from? It was derived from cotton-picking women who had to take their babies to work with them back in the day. They would fashion makeshift pacifiers by tying up sugar (cane) in a hanky for the babies to suck on. We may not be able to tell you what inspired Mel Gibson to address a female police officer as "Sugar Tits" during his DUI arrest back in 2006, but at least we came through for you in the revelation of how this South Carolina community got its name.

THE OFFICE GIRLS, ANTARCTICA

Here's a geographic location with a name that may seem to have the potential to come off as a feminist affront, but the bottom line on this lands pretty much on the up and up. The Office Girls are two glacial islands in Antarctica, about seven miles away from Welcome Mountain near the Southern Ocean coast.

We've got an inside tip here for those of you who may not have already figured it out on your own; the Welcome Mountain name seems to be purposefully misleading. If you've never been there, don't fall for the travel brochures where the offer of "free parking" is a total scam. If your ice-breaking ship is powerful enough to ram its way into the harbor, rest assured, no one is checking the parking stubs on the way out.

There are so many tiny pieces of land to map in Antarctica that the U.S. has an Advisory Committee on Antarctic Names to name them all, and in 1970 they chose "The Office Girls" for these two islands as a tribute to all of the home-based personnel who assisted with the administrative side of the missions from home in the continental U.S.

TITTY HILL, ENGLAND

Located 25 miles south of Portsmouth on the southern shores of England lies the small hamlet of Titty Hill, population 11. Surrounded by a patchwork of fields, the hamlet consists of a couple of houses and a farm called, appropriately enough, Titty Hill Farm.

Early in the first millennium, Titty Hill served as a mansio for the Roman Empire. A mansio was an official stopping point for government officials and military personnel.

Not a lot going on there these days, but if you'd like to leisurely lay back and listen to the waves of the English Channel lap up on the shores of Titty Hill Beach, this could be the spot for you. Another titillating

Titty Hill tidbit… it's a great place to base yourself for trips to nearby Wetwang and Shitterton.

> *Roman conquest was a shitty pill*
> *For England to swallow, but 'twill*
> *Inspire the Brits*
> *To show us their tits*
> *And go rename their town Titty Hill*

LAKE TITICACA, PERU/BOLIVIA

This is our hands-down winner for the one lake on the surface of the planet that is the funnest to say. If you're not familiar with the name the pronunciation would be "Tit-ee-kah-kah." If you're not giggling on the outside we know that you are within. Sure, it's sophomoric as hell, but when you can combine boobs and poop in one lake you might as well have some fun with it.

In our constant effort to inform as well as entertain, here's the lowdown on the lake. Straddling the border between Peru and Bolivia, Lake Titicaca is the 15th largest lake in the world and, at an elevation of 12,507 feet, is often called the "highest navigable lake" in the world. The "highest navigable lake" claim is generally considered to refer to commercial craft. Numerous smaller bodies of water around the world are at higher elevations. With depths up to 1,000 feet, this Andes Mountains lake is also one of the deepest in the world.

FLOATING ISLANDS - Here's the coolest Titicaca fun fact our research uncovered that we had never heard about before. Currently there are about 125 manmade floating islands inhabited by the Uros people, an ethnic group which has literally lived on the lake for centuries. They originally hit the water as a method to escape the Incas who were becoming more aggressively powerful in the first half of the last millennium.

But once afloat, the fun became contagious for the Uros and, believe it or not, there are still hundreds of them floating around Lake Titicaca as you're reading this. Granted, things have changed in the modern era. Not surprisingly, life gets much easier when you don't have armies of angry Incas hurling spears in your direction.

Irony of irony, the Uros outlived the Incas in a case we'll categorize under karma. So that victory being achieved, how does this floating island thing work in the 21st century and why do these Uros not just come inside and enjoy the plumbing? The sadly ironic thought that occurs to us as we compose this piece in the age of Covid-19 is that the Uros are among the few people on the planet blissfully ignorant of the fact that the toilet paper at the local market is always sold out.

At one point in the mid-20th century, the Uros' lifestyle was trending toward termination. The number of floating islands had decreased to 60 and, tradition notwithstanding, their people were beginning to opt for a more traditional lifestyle. If you recall the number from a few paragraphs ago, Lake Titicaca is currently the home of 125 floating Uros' islands. So what happened to cause the crazy comeback? In a word, capitalism,

The Uros realized that the Titicaca tourism trade was something that could be used to their economic advantage. Awash in natural beauty, the lake is one of South America's most popular tourist attractions. The Uros initially entered the business world with the sale of their traditional crafts as souvenirs. Then they were struck by a total flash of genius.

They started building new islands as floating hotels. The idea took off, with many tourists enticed by the experience of spending the night like the natives had done centuries ago. Some of the hotels have achieved virtual luxury status with generators providing electricity and rental options available for everything from paddleboats to motorboats to water skiing equipment. And the best news is there's nary a viable threat posed by the Incas these days.

At any rate, returning to the Uros story, their floating islands are made of totora reeds that grow in the shallow parts of the lake. The islands themselves are made up of layers upon layers of the reeds. As the layers closest to the water begin to rot, they are replaced with fresh reeds on top. While the totora reeds have always been the base material for the formation of the Uros' islands, as time went on they developed the ability to turn their reed handiwork into furniture and shelters.

Here's the etymology of Titicaca. In Aymaran, a language family that calls the central Andes home, "titi" translates to "puma" and "caca" means "gray," while in Quechua, another local language, it means "rock."

In English, "titi" is probably not something you should put in a Google image search at work, and in Spanish "caca" means "poop," but they weren't speaking English or Spanish back when they named the lake. The actual translation is something along the lines of "The Gray Puma" or "Rock of the Puma."

NIPPLE PEAK, ANTARCTICA

One of the northernmost points on the continent, Nipple Peak is located on the Antarctica peninsula that stretches up toward South America. If you think the Belgians shot their wad when they found the Congo, you'd be sadly mistaken. Nipple Peak was discovered by the 1897–1899 Belgian Antarctic Expedition. It was the British however who bestowed the erotic name upon the mountain when they mapped the place in 1944. If you're a numbers person, it is 2,215 feet up to the tip of the nipple.

Noting the subtle change of one vowel in the second word of this entry, allow us to espouse the theory that despite the arousingly provocative pun suggested by the name of this mountain, no matter how close you are to your partner, it would be a difficult location in which to share a Nipple Peek. It's colder than a witch's tit up there.

Chapter 6
COCK-A-DOODLE-DOO

In our drive for gender equality we're going to move on over to the males for this next chapter. For all you guys out there be prepared for the fact that the news is going to range from "that feels so good" to "that hurts like hell."

On the upside, we will be giving you a **Wetwang** and on the downside you'll feel what it's like to get a **Kick In de Kök**. You may be able to avoid the good and the bad by simply wearing a **Condom**. We'll take you there first.

A Kick in the Cock is rejection
A Condom provides some protection
Look for your next bang
And get a Wet Wang
Resulting in your New Erection

CONDOM, FRANCE

If you're in the mood for that type of thing there's a History of Contraception Museum outside Toronto which is probably closer, but your experience would seem to be more authentic if you could make it to the Condom Museum in Condom. The city of 7,000 is located in southwest France and it has a good story to tell about its museum.

A dude named Gerard Dubrac runs a local pharmacy and when visitors keep asking for his shop's stamp on condom boxes, he decides there is some notoriety – and money – to be made off the town's name. "Why not a condom museum?" the pharmacist thinks.

So he pitches the idea to the town officials who scoff at it. But when it comes to curious sexual ingenuity, everyone knows you don't fuck with the French. How does Dubrac respond to the rebuke? He runs for mayor and wins. Condom Museum? Come on down!

BLUE BALL, PENNSYLVANIA

Geographically speaking, Blue Ball's not far from Intercourse and Bird-in-Hand. Oh the irony of the names of some of these towns in the Amish country of Pennsylvania! This town of about 1,000 people is located in the southeastern part of the state.

The name is derived from the Blue Ball Hotel which was built in the early 1700's. The proprietor hung a blue ball in front of the place which came to be known as "The sign of the blue ball." So this part can be a bit confusing because what they were referring to as a "sign" was not literally a sign, it was literally a ball. At any rate, the name caught on and "Blue Ball" became the name of first, the hotel, and later the entire town.

KICK IN DE KÖK, ESTONIA

This is perhaps the most painfully excruciating of all of our entries, at least for the gentlemen in our audience. Kick In de Kök is the name of the area surrounding an artillery tower in Tallinn, Estonia which was built in 1475. On the subject of pain, please allow us to share this additional fun fact. Cannon balls dating back to 1577 are still embedded in the outer walls of this Tallinn tower. At that point in time the area which is modern-day Estonia, was part of the German-speaking Prussian Empire.

That leads us to the explanation of the etymology of this quirky name. In German, the phrase Kick In de Kök was generally applied to military towers used for surveillance purposes. The literal translation, which doesn't seem to mesh with the military usage, was "peep in the kitchen" and the general point was to use a high vantage point to observe your surroundings.

And for what it's worth, "peep in the kitchen" sounds much less painful than the image conjured up when a guy hears "Kick In de Kök."

NEW ERECTION, VIRGINIA

New Erection is a small town located in northwest Virginia. The community took its name from a Presbyterian church called "New

Erection," so named because it was re-erected there, having previously been located at Dayton.

Not a lot of storyline here, so we'll use it as a springboard to share one of our favorite stories from our second book.

DAYTON & EATON ~ This is a story shared with us by a close colleague who grew up in New Lebanon, Ohio which is halfway between Dayton and Eaton. He often talked about how tough it was growing up in New Lebanon. Why, do you ask?

Here's the reason he said that it's tough to grow up in a small town halfway between Dayton and Eaton. Whenever he went out with a girl he could never remember if he was datin' a girl from Eaton, or eatin' a girl from Dayton. Life is tough in New Lebanon, Ohio.

WETWANG, EAST YORKSHIRE, ENGLAND

Located in the northeastern corner of the country, Wetwang is a village of about 750 people. Douglas Adams (author of *Hitchhiker's Guide to the Galaxy*) and John Lloyd (producer of the television series) have officially designated 'wetwang' as 'moist penis' in their 1983 dictionary spoof *The Meaning of Liff*. Two less exciting theories are offered for the unusual name.

Theory #1 ~ It's based upon an Old English word meaning, "field for the trial of a legal action."

Theory #2 ~ It's based upon a slang expression for "wet field."

A tradition has been established whereby the town appoints an honorary mayor based upon comedy performances on British television. Obviously, with a name like Wetwang, there is a vast potential to reap comedic value.

CHAPTER 7
WHAT'S UP, PUSSYCAT?

Remember the James Taylor song "Carolina in my Mind"? In a live show recorded in 1995 he joked that the line running through his head when he originally wrote the song was "Nothing could be finer, than to be in Carolina in the morning." Then, as men sometimes do, he allowed his sexual head to go sideways for a moment and the rhyme running through his head became, "Nothing could be finer than to be in your vagina in the morning." Morphing those two storylines, genius James gathered his thoughts and penned one of his all-time classics.

Right now we'd love to hear the artistry that could have been manifested if James Taylor had followed through on his original thought to write the vagina song. Nobody could have walked the gender tight wire like J.T. Only James Taylor could have written a dude song about pussies that chicks would have loved to dance to.

But we diverge. Time to stop pussy-footing around and get back to the book. This will be an adventurous chapter. You will find out what it's like to be caught up **Pussy Creek** without a paddle. We'll take you from the land of **Muff** to the town of **Twatt**. And in the ultimate fantasy you'll find out what it's like to complete one **Beaverlick** only to discover it's time to immediately move on to the **Big Beaver**.

Beaverlick, it does have a mystique
Those Muff divers love Pussy Creek
Hats off to the Scots
Cause they have two Twatts
Pussy, France we salute tongue-in-cheek

BEAVERLICK, KENTUCKY

Obviously the double entendre goddess was smiling down upon us when we stumbled across this one. Actually that smile would have been even bigger if we'd started this article a couple centuries ago. When it was initially founded as a fur trading site in 1780 it was called Big Beaver Lick.

Beaverlick is located in the north central part of Kentucky, so far north in fact that it is considered part of the Metropolitan area of Cincinnati, Ohio. During the era when fur trading was actually a thing, Beaverlick became a fairly bustling little town. At its peak in 1850, the community grew to have a general store, carriage maker, hotel, flour mill, hat shop, two blacksmiths, two physicians and three churches. The post office operated from 1854–1944.

But by 1900 the population had dwindled to about 50 and Beaverlick was fading into fur-trading obscurity. Today not much is left of this small village except historic houses, churches and cemeteries.

Beaverlick seems to have been a conservative community. Our research turned up the following article on the September 16, 1879 issue of the *Beaverlick Banner*. The paper described the town by saying, *"Beaverlick is one of the most quiet villages on earth, especially on the Sabbath, though two shops are dealing out the deadly drug on weekdays. Thanks be to God and honor to the proprietors, not one drop is sold here on Sunday. We owe it to William Rex Robinson, who came and lectured to us until, with tears in their eyes, proprietors of liquor promised him they'd vend no more on Sunday."*

To be certain, the fun with wordplay never ends in Beaverlick. Would you be surprised if we told you that the town got its name because it was on the Beaver Branch of Big Bone Creek?

BIG BEAVER, SASKATCHEWAN, CANADA

For a community that registered an official population of 15 in the 2006 Canadian census, we surprisingly found three unique stories here. That could be a record for our series on quirky geography names – we're thinking we have not previously written about a place that averages one great story for every 5 people. Here we go.

#1) The mayor of Big Beaver is Woody March. There's an obvious joke in there that, as small town newspaper writers, we're going to let you write on your own.

#2) If you drive south from Big Beaver towards Montana you cross from the Central Time Zone and a community which converts to daylight savings time into a community in the Mountain Time Zone which does not convert to daylight savings time. So as you cross that specific boundary you instantaneously add two hours to your life. Just in case the story has you so enticed that you are about to head to Saskatchewan to find your fountain of youth, please be advised, this time travel trick just works once.

#3) Big Beaver is referenced in Warren Zevon's song "Hit Somebody (The Hockey Song)" from his 2002 album *My Ride's Here*. The track was about a hockey player born in Big Beaver and had a couple celebrity side notes. It featured vocals by David Letterman and was co-written by Zevon and Mitch Albom, author of *Tuesdays with Morrie* and *The Five People You Meet in Heaven*.

Thus concludes our hat trick of hilarity related to Big Beaver, Canada.

PUSSY, FRANCE

Pussy is a small town in southeastern France not far from the border with Italy. And if this town's name wasn't already something you'd like to pet, we've got more good news for you. It's bisected by a river called the Torrent of Pussy. Can't we all just feel the flow?

The town's name derives from the Roman name Pussius, but don't bother telling the tourists that because they're all having too much fun. While the tourists continue to come into Pussy – let's face it, who wouldn't want to have their photo snapped by the big Pussy sign? – the natives are pouring out of Pussy in droves.

The Pussy population plummeted from 1,455 in 1561, to 548 in 1776, to 276 in 1979. The fact that the French are giving up on this Pussy so readily seems to repudiate their romantic reputation, but the numbers don't lie.

PUSSY CREEK, NEW ZEALAND

Pussy Creek flows in central New Zealand. If you're enough of a geography geek to know the basic layout of that country, it's in the northern part of the South Island.

Conveying the concept that we should all maintain our sense of optimism about the possibilities of a wet pussy, we would like to share with you the fact that Pussy Creek empties into the Hope River.

BIMBO, CENTRAL AFRICAN REPUBLIC

The Central African Republic's second largest city, Bimbo is located in the far south of the country right on the border with the Congo Democratic Republic. The one thing that caught our attention about this one was the prison system.

Call it African irony if you will, but the city is the site of the country's only sex-segregated women's prison. It's almost like the powers that be asked themselves, "Where can we send these female criminals that will denigrate them even further?" And the answer of course was, "Let's send these bimbos to Bimbo."

MUFF, IRELAND

Muff is a small port town, population about 1,300, located in northwestern Ireland, right on the border with Northern Ireland, which is actually another country. In our British geography review we'll share the fact that the United Kingdom consists of four countries: England, Scotland, Wales and Northern Ireland. The first three of those four countries are on the main Island of Great Britain.

The other island contains Northern Ireland (UK) and the separate country of Ireland. Muff is significant politically and geographically as one of the most northerly border crossing points between the Republic of Ireland and Northern Ireland.

Every summer, during the first week of August, the town hosts the annual Muff Festival which sounds like a lot of fun. Activities include all kinds of music, parades, parties, copious beer consumption and a variety of bizarre competitions including pig racing and lorry (truck) pulling events.

Let's face it, if it were not for one specific cunnilingus cliché this town never would have made the book. That being said, if you ever hit this town, you'll be happy to know they do have a sanctioned Muff Diving Club.

VAGINA, RUSSIA

Not that it's a place where you wouldn't feel like you'd want to come, for a couple reasons we feel like the folks in Vagina, Russia are just jacking us around a little bit. Before we get into the heart of the matter, here's a quick background. The town is located in the province of Kurganskaya in western Siberia, and has a few hundred inhabitants.

Here are two examples to validate our premise that the people of Vagina are yanking our chains. Why do we think they're screwing with us?

Reason #1 - Feel free to try this at home. Go to Google and enter "Things to do in Vagina, Kurganskaya Oblast', Russia / Facebook." Click on that "Things to do in Vagina" option and the first thing you see is "No Recommended Places to Eat." What, do they think we have a one-track mind?

Reason #2 - There are multiple places in the world that have names which are scandalous words in English. For example you have Anus, France; Fucking, Austria; and Kick In de Kök, Estonia. The storylines behind the names of those places are all basically the same. They were named a long time ago, don't mean the same thing in the native tongue as they do in English, and there was no knowledge that the chosen name had any particular meaning in another language.

Think about it; if you're herding your sheep in Austria around the year 800 and trying to come up for a name of your town, who gives a fuck what the English are saying? Only in our global age of the internet did some things like this come to people's attention and all of the aforementioned towns have kept their original names, a decision with which we concur. Why compromise a thousand years of history and tradition just because coincidentally your name happens to mean something different in another language?

But here's the arousing aspect about Vagina. They changed their name from Kolkhoz to Vagina, and they did it in 1991. That happened to be the year of the dissolution of the USSR but we don't know if that really had anything to do with it. Any way you look at it, by 1991 you would think the people on the naming committee would have done a better job of putting their finger on the pulse of the issue. Or perhaps there was some consensual sexual collusion reflected by the hanky-panky arising in this Russian version of the name game.

We're going to leave you with the following question and a list of options as to how the response should be finished. Prepare yourself for a flurry of clichés and euphemisms. Did the people who adopted the name of Vagina in 1991 make this move on purpose or were they…

- Pussy-footing around
- Watching too many episodes of *Leave it to Beaver*
- Beating around the bush
- Getting caught with their pants down
- Parting the pink sea
- Listening to their Hairy Manilow records.
- Putting ranch dressing in the Hidden Valley

TWATT, SCOTLAND

If Scotland wasn't already your favorite country, it will be soon. Believe it or not, the Scots have two Twatts. Yep, there are only two geographic locations on the planet called "Twatt" and they're both in Scotland. Here Kitty, Kitty.

There's one Twatt on the Orkney Islands and another on the Shetland Islands, and both of them will leave you wanting to cream your Twinkie (Feel free to add this euphemism to the list above.) If you hit the internet looking for the Top 10 Things to do in either Twatt, our extensive research reveals that #1 on the list is stand next to the road sign with an arrow pointing your way.

Before we tackle the etymology, we'll differentiate one Twatt from the other, a skill we've spent a lifetime refining. The Twatt in the Shetland Islands is the bigger one, sometimes preferable, as it has a few hundred inhabitants. It also had a post office from 1879-2002 and there are remains from a WWII airfield there as well.

If you'd prefer a smaller, tighter Twatt community, head for the Orkney Islands. Their population comes in at under a hundred.

The name of both settlements originates from an Old Norse word meaning "small parcel of land." Of course the name wouldn't have shown up in this book if it weren't a homophone for the word "twat" (one "t") meaning vagina. Fully analyzing the etymology angle we should go on to acknowledge that "twat" is also used in English to mean a weak or contemptible individual.

So with that in mind, next time you find yourself vacationing in the Scottish Isles, don't pose by the Twatt sign unless your level of self-confidence sufficiently supports the pose. People could take this picture two ways.

Here's our final thoughts on this tale of two Twatts. If you're at the point where you're ready to stop reading and take in a movie, we have a suggestion for you. How about cueing up a little James Bond and watching *Goldfinger*? That's the one, if you recall, where the female lead is named Pussy Galore.

CHAPTER 8
THE JOY OF SEX

This will be for sure the best fucking chapter in the book. It's actually in Austria, **Fucking**, that is. It's a true town with a titillating tale. How should you determine if you'd like to continue with this chapter? Please allow our next sentence of wordplay to become your litmus test regarding your continuance. Keep reading if...

You'd like to see a **Spread Eagle - Virgin - Come By Chance** in **Horneytown**; it might be a **Tightsqueeze** but **Blow Me Down** that **Bimbo** will **Sexmoan** before her **Climax** during **Intercourse**. There's also the part where you get to put the **Dildo** in the **Vagina** of the **Hooker** while she's performing **Oral**. And after that deed is done you can relax, kick back, and watch your favorite episode of *The Big Bang Theory*, **Pennycomequick**.

COME BY CHANCE, NEWFOUNDLAND, CANADA

Sometimes that's the best way to do it. This town of just a few hundred people is located in the province of Newfoundland which is an island off the eastern coast of Canada. The first use of the name was recorded in 1706 with no explanation of the derivation. The only theory we saw floated was the notion that the harbor was discovered by chance.

Come by Chance did produce one hockey player who made it to the NHL. Bob Gladney spent time with both the Pittsburgh Penguins and Los Angeles Kings.

DILDO, NEWFOUNDLAND, CANADA

Dildo is a small town of 250 people located on the island of Newfoundland which, as we stated in the previous entry, is off the east coast of Canada. It's been around for centuries but through the magic of television Jimmy Kimmel provided Dildo with its proverbial 15 minutes of fame just within the past few years. Actually it turned into more like a week of fame, but more on that later.

The origin of Dildo's name is uncertain. Dildo is located on the coast of a phallus-shaped peninsula initially giving credence to the theory that the name of the town was based upon the shape of the peninsula. But in our research we came across the fact that the first occurrence upon which the town was referred to as Dildo came in 1711. That revelation sent us into a sideways research project into the etymology of the word dildo and exactly what it meant over 300 years ago.

Our first and most basic discovery was that, at the time, "dildo" could mean any cylindrical object, from nautical pins to test tubes. But a deeper dive also revealed the following. We found three equally feasible theories that could be used to support a sexual connotation to the theory that Dildo's name could have had phallic foundations.

#1) We'll look to Italian eroticism on this first one. The 1650's first featured the use of the word "diletto" in Italian, meaning "a woman's delight."

#2) In the early 1600's the word "dill-doll" came into use in English. That word was deemed as having been derived from the old Norse word "dilla", a verb meaning "to soothe."

#3) And this may be our choice as the most likely possibility of the three in the running. With an English derivation, there was a phrase that referred to a man's penis as used in the 17th century ballad "The Maid's Complaint for want of a Dil Doul," which was likely a real toe-tapper of a tune at the time.

The name of the town has frequently become a source of celebrity, some of which has been endearing and some of which has been embarrassing. In the 20th century there were several campaigns to change the name, though all failed. Probably a good thing; history should always trump hysteria.

Any possibility of a name change was certainly put to rest in August of 2019 when the late-night talk show *Jimmy Kimmel Live!* made Dildo the focus of attention over a number of shows. As part of the series, host Jimmy Kimmel was made honorary mayor of Dildo (the community is governed by a volunteer committee and does not have an elected mayor). Guillermo Rodriguez, who serves as Kimmel's sidekick "security guard," was made an honorary citizen of Dildo through the Newfoundland tradition of "Screeching-In," on the August 15, 2019 broadcast of the show.

That Screech-In tradition is a Newfoundland ceremony where they give CFA's (Come From Away's) the prestigious title of honorary Newfoundlanders. Think of it as a fun rite of initiation. Typically, the CFA's are made to repeat some local sayings, kiss a cod fish, drink some Screech rum, and possibly try some Newfoundland Steak.

Following the Screech-In, Rodriguez visited the community for a week. Kimmel, declared Hollywood to be Dildo's sister city. As part of his grandiose gesture, he also gifted the community with a giant "DILDO" sign (in the style of the classic "HOLLYWOOD" sign) which sits on the hillside overlooking the Canadian community.

At this point the conservatives in the community who had previously lobbied for a name change had to be conquered. The only thing worse than having a huge Dildo sign looming large over your hamlet's horizon would be the dire situation of having no current explanation of what it's there for.

BLOW ME DOWN, NEWFOUNDLAND, CANADA

Seems like Newfoundland must be a particularly promiscuous province. This component completes the hat trick of horniness for these crazy Canadians. After you've Come By Chance with your Dildo, it's time to finish things off with some oral sex in Blow Me Down!

The classic character with whom we most associate this command would be the seafaring Popeye. Whenever the mighty sailing man found himself in a surprising situation he would utter the command, "Well, blow me down!" If you ever happen to find yourself in this location in Newfoundland, Canada, don't lose time looking for the "Home of Popeye" sign.

The name is derived from the fact that it's windy as hell on this small peninsula located at the mouth of the Bay of Islands. If you fend off the wind, there's really only one thing to do while you're here. This spot on the west coast of Newfoundland Island is home to the Blow Me Down Provincial Park.

ORGY, FRANCE

Here's a town that operates upon the premise the more the merrier, a theme perpetuated by the photo ops taken at the town sign. Orgy is located 92 miles southeast of Paris and, if you're interested, just 20 miles south of Anus. The French liked the name so much they also assigned it to a Vietnamese village during the era when French Indochina was a territory of France.

PHUKET, THAILAND

If you live in Thailand and you're looking at booking the celebration of a birthday, wedding, anniversary, or any other big event you could literally say, "Fuck it, I'm going to Phuket," and actually mean it. Phuket is a rainforested, mountainous island in the Andaman Sea, which has some of Thailand's most popular beaches, mainly situated along the clear waters of the island's western shore.

Amongst the nodding palm trees, glittering seas and lively towns, there are plenty of partying options, as well as a wide range of activities available. These include everything from a serene cruise around the main island, to an exhilarating speedboat trip to nearby smaller islands, to elephant rides back on the main island of Phuket.

> *There once was a man from Nantucket*
> *Whose Orgy in Dildo, he ducked it*
> *Come By Chance, no not he*
> *Opted out for plan B*
> *Went to Thailand and visited Phuket*

HOOKER, OKLAHOMA

This small city of 2,000 people has a unique location in the Sooner State, being in one of the three counties that comprise the panhandle of Oklahoma. That puts it in the far western part of the state and it's a short drive north to Kansas or south to Texas.

The city was named in honor of a cattle rancher named John "Hooker" Threlkeld. In 1873, he was one of the first people to start running cattle in the 40 mile-wide area that was initially labeled "undesirable territory." Threlkeld earned the nickname Hooker because of his reputation as one of the best cattle ropers of his time.

There are a few examples of the community having fun with the potentially risqué town name. The mascot for Hooker's sports teams is the Horny Frogs. One note of specificity on this nickname tends to indicate the Hooker folks are having fun with their horny frogs. Texas Christian University, for example, has the Horned Toads as the school's mascot. But, for the record, the frogs in Hooker are not horned, they're horny.

For our second example we'll defer to the town motto. Residents of Hooker would like to remind you, "It's a location, not a vocation." Clearly they're having some fun with it.

CLIMAX, COLORADO

Climax, Colorado was a small town whose time has come and gone. At one time this mining village was the highest town in America but now it sits as an abandoned ghost town while the mine churns on. We'll explain the "highest-town" reference shortly, but rest assured, there are no drug connections.

During its glory days the Climax mine produced three-quarters of the world's molybdenum which is a chemical element used in the manufacture of structural steel, stainless steel, and cast iron. Because it has the sixth-highest melting point of any element, it is useful in environments of intense heat, such as military armor, aircraft parts, and industrial motors.

Climax is located along the Continental Divide at an elevation of 11,360 feet and at the point in time when people lived there it was the highest human settlement in the United States. In terms of permanent residences Climax, the old town that sat at the top of America, was abandoned in 1965 and all the houses deemed worthy of salvaging were moved to Leadville, Colorado.

But the commercial buildings are still standing in this modern-day ghost town which does provide Climax with a quirky tourist appeal. If you want to get your picture taken in front of the highest-ever U.S. post office, train station or hospital that's a goal which can only be climaxed in Climax.

INTERCOURSE, PENNSYLVANIA

Oh the irony! How did a home to the virtuous Amish get such a name? The village, which was founded in 1754, was first named Cross Keys after a local tavern. Its name was changed to Intercourse in 1814. Located in southeastern Pennsylvania, Intercourse has a population of about 1,300.

There are three competing theories as to the origin of the name with no clear favorite.

Theory #1 - One story ties it to a horse racetrack that used to exist just east of the town. The entrance to the track had a sign above it that read "Enter Course." Locals began to refer to the town as "Entercourse," which eventually evolved into "Intercourse."

Theory #2 - The town may have been named after its location at the intersection — or "intercourse" of two primary roads from back in the day. The Old King's Highway from Philadelphia to Pittsburgh — now Old Philadelphia Pike — ran east/west through the center of the town. The road from Wilmington, Delaware to Erie, Pennsylvania ran through town in the north/south direction.

Theory #3 - Back in the day, the word "intercourse" was commonly used to describe the "fellowship" and "social interaction and support" shared in the community of faith. This camaraderie was woven into the identity of the community and may have influenced the naming of the town.

There have been multiple examples of Intercourse being referenced in pop culture. As seen in our list of theories above, we like to work in threes, so here is our trio of pop culture examples.

Example #1 - In a recurring segment that aired with the title, "What's Wrong with These Photos?" *The Ellen DeGeneres Show* garnered laughs with a picture of an actual Pennsylvania road sign saying, "Welcome to Intercourse."

Example #2 ~ Kay Lenz's titular character in the 1973 film *Breezy* reveals that she is from Intercourse. ("I've heard all the jokes," she tells William Holden, "and you have to pass through Faithful to get there.")

Example #3 ~ In *The Simpsons* episode titled, "The Old Man and the 'C' Student," it was revealed that Superintendent Chalmers lived in Intercourse.

KISSING, BAVARIA, GERMANY

Kissing is a municipality in the province of Bavaria, in southern Germany, with about 11,000 inhabitants. It is located about 300 miles south of Berlin. The etymology of Kissing was first documented in 1050 A.D. when it showed up as the town of *Chissingin*. The surname Kissinger (as in Henry Kissinger) means inhabitant of Kissing or Kissingen.

HUMPTULIPS, WASHINGTON

Okay, if Fucktheflowers doesn't work for you, perhaps this could be your backup. Located in the northwest corner of Washington, Humptulips is a small town of about 250 people. When you drive by the welcome sign, the town has one of those quirky names that residents say they are always asked about. Humptulips natives are quick to dispel any notion that fragrant flowers are being inappropriately abused in any local greenhouse shenanigans.

The town got its name from a totally-innocent-sounding Native American phrase meaning "hard to pole." Interpret that expression as you will, but it's likely our Indian friends were referring to the difficulty they had poling their canoes up the river in the area. Tulips everywhere will sleep more comfortably tonight.

PENNYCOMEQUICK, DEVON, ENGLAND

We'll give you a multiple choice question on this one. Located in southern England, Pennycomequick is which of the following?

A) An area within the city of Plymouth, England.

B) A name which came from a Celtic phrase meaning "head of a wooded valley."

C) The place name that could have been the title of your favorite episode ever of *The Big Bang Theory*.

D) All of the above.

(As fate would have it, our word count for the above entry came in at 69. Count them if you'd like. Oh, and by the way, the correct answer is D.)

Humptulips does sound rather sick
We do much prefer Beaverlick
Before our Wet Wang
We'll watch the Big Bang
Episode that we love "Pennycomequick"

ORAL, SOUTH DAKOTA

Oral is a small town in southwest South Dakota with a population of 192. Just how rural the community is can be conveyed by the fact that the town's few hundred people are spread out in such a way that the population density calculates at 2 people per square mile.

The post office opened there in 1894 and there are two competing theories as to the etymology of the name.

- Some say Oral has the middle name of the first postmaster's son.
- Others believe the community was so named with the expectation the place would become something people would be talking about.

We're not sure which theory about the origin of the name is right, but we can be sure that the aspiration suggested by the second theory is wrong. Not a lot of people are talking about Oral these days.

TIGHTSQUEEZE, VIRGINIA

Just what are the residents of this town trying to squeeze through? Alas, nothing too erotic. This town is located in south central Virginia not far from the border with North Carolina. How did Tightsqueeze get its unusual name? Here's the scoop.

In 1870, a general store was opened by W.H. Colbert, in what was clearly an era before any zoning laws were in effect. Colbert built his store extremely close to the edge of the road so that women riding in carriages could get out from the vehicles directly onto the porch of his store without getting muddy or dusty.

Shortly thereafter, another merchant named Isaiah Giles built a blacksmith-wheelwright shop directly across the road from the general store. It, too, was on the road's edge. Due to the closeness of the two buildings, people traveling through the area in buggies and wagons had to slow down as they passed between the two.

After having successfully made the pass, these travelers began to warn others coming from the other direction of the tight squeeze they would soon be facing ahead. Upon the constant repetition of the warning, "tight squeeze," the name stuck and eventually morphed into just one word.

We're sure that when you began reading this entry, having become accustomed to our style and predispositions, you were probably flipping a coin and thinking, "This 'Tightsqueeze' thing is 50-50. They're either going to be writing about something really dangerous or writing about sex. Time to place my bet."

Well, sorry to disappoint you. We're sorry nobody got laid or killed in Tightsqueeze. We'll try to make it up to you in the future.

SPREAD EAGLE, WISCONSIN

First, you need to get your mind out of the gutter. The positioning of the lakes in this town is what gave Spread Eagle its name. From an aerial perspective, the chain of lakes in the town resembles an eagle with its wings spread. The town is located in northeastern Wisconsin.

HORNEYTOWN, NORTH CAROLINA

This small town, with a population of just 15, is located in central North Carolina about 25 miles west of Greensboro. The quirky name has a simple explanation which has nothing to do with the libidos of the residents. The earliest settlers of the area were the Horney family and the town came to bear that name.

As small as it is, the town manages to straddle two counties, Forsyth and Davidson, so those are the jurisdictions which share the dilemma that hangs over Horneytown. What would that problem be?

Sex fiends from all corners of the globe converge on Horneytown in hopes of being able to steal one of the town signs. Let's face it, who wouldn't want one of those babies hanging on their wall when a young romantic brings home that all important prospective partner after a successful first date?

With the rate of sign theft landing at a level of one every two months, county officials have decided to take a new approach. A recent article we read reported the addition of a secondary sign in blue, telling would-be thieves that the signs are tracked by GPS. Skeptics that we are, we couldn't help but wonder if the GPS devices were actually installed or if the new blue signs are just a ploy to instill fear in potential thieves.

Right now we have our crack research team investigating this situation and working on the possibility of bringing one of the #1 most-stolen road signs in the state of North Carolina back home to New York. If this doesn't work out, we do have a couple of backup plans.

We could shoot for one of the second-most-stolen signs in NC. What's #2 on the list, you ask? That would be "Rolling Green" a must for all the stoners in the state. Our other backup plan? If things don't work out in Horneytown, we will be just 26 miles away from the town of Climax and 47 miles from the town of Erect. Travel planning for us is an addiction.

SEXMOAN, PHILIPPINES

This city of 28,000 people is located in the province of Pampanga, Philippines. Named by Spanish friars, the name in the original Filipino language meant "meeting place" or "meeting point." Obviously, the Spanish holy men who bestowed the moniker had never even had sex, let alone moaned during it. They were oblivious to any kind of English translation which might take on sexual connotations.

Of course the concept of place names taking on unwanted sexual connotations because the wording had a different meaning, in a different language, has been a frequent occurrence in this book. But in the vast majority of situations, tradition prevails and the community sticks with its historic name.

For example, Fucking, Austria kept Fucking; France has held onto Pussy, Anus, Condom and Orgy. Scotland had two Twatts and kept them both. That however was not the case in Sexmoan. On January 15, 1991 Sexmoan officially changed its name to Sasmuan. The change in spelling is essentially a reflection of how the name was actually pronounced in the Filipino language. Thus bringing an end to the sex in Sexmoan.

FUCKING, AUSTRIA

Sure it's a tough name to live with but since 1994 the town has held three votes regarding a name replacement, and not a fucking thing has changed. The village has a population of just a few hundred and is located in northwest Austria 21 miles north of Salzburg and just 2.5 miles east of the Inn River, which forms the border with Germany. By the way, that figure on the population does not include the steady stream of tourists and thrill seekers who frequent Fucking to get their picture taken by the sign.

SIGN OF THE TIMES ~ On the subject of signs there's much to be said. Let's face it, as a conversation starter who wouldn't want to have one of these hanging in your humble home? So for just that reason the signs were regularly ripped off. When the 2004 vote to change the name failed, it went down with a rider clause that the signs were to be remodeled as theft-resistant.

So while they're no longer being stolen, the signs do still contribute to the town's lifestyle. In addition to the influx of folks just taking regular pictures by the signs, it's probably not too surprising to hear that there have been multiple examples of both men and women removing layers of clothing to add an element of erotic enhancement to their pose by the sign.

Then of course there's the ultimate pose which has been achieved by only the most daring celebrities of sign sensationalism. There are documented cases of couples copulating for the camera just below the Fucking sign. When it comes to that ultimate sign soiree photo, for some folks it's either go big or stay at home.

OKAY, LET'S VOTE ON THIS ~ So with such shameless shenanigans shagging at every entrance to town it's not shocking that some folks fancied foregoing 1200 years of Fucking and changing the name of the town. Here's the timeline on that story. The first town referendum took place in 1994.

The situation was lamented by then-Mayor Siegfried Hoeppel who pointed out the fact that, "Town signs have been stolen seven times in the last few months. With signs costing several hundred dollars apiece, much of our town's budget is being spent replacing the signs." He went on to express his hope that, "Hopefully further thefts will be avoided through the use of increased concrete and… bigger screws." Honest to God we couldn't make this shit up!

2004 VOTE ~ The next vote occurred in 2004 after Franz Meindl had taken over as the new mayor. It's interesting to note Mayor Meindl's shift in stance between this vote and the subsequent one in 2012. As the feisty new mayor in 2004 Meindl issued the following statement on the vote to change the town's name. "Everyone here knows what it means in English," Meindl said, "but for us Fucking is Fucking and it's going to stay Fucking." Powerful words if ever any were spoken.

Over the (inter)course of the next 8 years Meindl apparently saw more people having sex under his sign than suited his fancy. And then there were the phone calls. Sure there's a bit of humor the first time you pick up the phone and your "hello" is greeted with the response, "Hi, are you the Fucking mayor?" followed by raucous laughter. But it's easy to see how that could get old fast and apparently that all took its toll on Mayor Meindl.

2012 VOTE ~ By the time of the 2012 vote, Meindl's message on the mess had been modified. "I always wanted the name to stay but it's just gotten to be too much now," Mayor Meindl said, "the only problem is that we need all the Fucking residents to agree on the name change; everyone needs to agree before it can happen."

Actually in his anxiety to advocate for his aspiration, Meindl overstated his objective. He didn't need everyone to agree; all he really needed was for a majority to agree. But alas, agreement was not in the cards for Meindl's mission. For the third time in three decades the Fuckingers said, "Fuck You" to the idea of a name change.

WHY, OH WHY? ~ All of which inevitably leads to the question of why. Our research led to a three-tonged-forking response:

#1) Austrians are stubborn. Their town had been named after the man who founded it in the 9th century. His name was Focko which morphed into the town name of Fucking almost a millennium before the etymology of the verb fuck first appeared in the English language in the 17th century. The Austrians frankly don't give a fuck about the fact that their town name has a meaning in English but has no meaning whatsoever in their native language.

#2) Austrians like money. The unusual place name brings people into town. Think about it; if you own a business in Fucking, know somebody that works at a business in Fucking, or know somebody who might inherit money from the sale of a business in Fucking; the quirky name is in your best financial interests.

#3) Austrians like sex. And some of them no longer have the means to enjoy it without assistance. We're going to end this piece with our favorite quote which turned up in our research. Fucking resident Helga Fritzenhopper has a home whose yard serves as the placement for one of the "Welcome to Fucking" signs. Certain that she had been inconvenienced by the phalanx of photo takers descending upon her property, Mayor Meindl approached her to ask her support for his "Vote Yes" on the name change campaign.

Her answer was "Fuck, No." When asked why, the old lady said, "I haven't had sex for the past 25 years since my husband Adolph died. With that Fucking sign in my yard, I get to see live sex half a dozen times a year. That's a pretty nice number because it actually about equals what I was getting when Adolph was alive and now I don't even have to wash the sheets." We'll actually add the obvious now. Some elderly Austrians are blessed with a great sense of humor.

Horneytown's found in North Carolina
France's Orgy was in Indochina
In Sexmoan they're sucking
While Austria's Fucking
Russia changes a name to Vagina

VIRGIN, UTAH

This town of about 600 people is located in southwestern Utah near Zion National Park. The first Europeans arrived here in 1857 and, as you might have heard, the Mormons weren't far behind, led by Brigham Young whose impressive marital scorecard landed with a total wife tally of 55.

How's this for irony? Brigham Young, or "Bring 'em Young" as the townsfolk often called him, chose Virgin, Utah to be the site of his organization of the United Order on March 4, 1871.

VIRGINVILLE, PENNSYLVANIA

Virginville is located in southeast Pennsylvania between Hershey and Philadelphia. The name may be a bit of a misnomer because with the population of around 300, they're clearly not all virgins.

CHAPTER 9
WORD PLAY

After spending the last chapter playing with the parts of our sexual partners, we're going to dial it down a notch and dedicate this chapter to some heavy word play. We'll show you how you can be in **Key West**, sorta, twice without leaving the Virginia Territory. We'll play **Truth or Consequences** and take you to the very end of the alphabet and just to show you that we haven't totally lost our sexual edge, we have multiple stories where people get off by establishing themselves as being the longest.

In Key West we could try vermouth
Eye for an eye and a tooth for a tooth
Or we could try sex
In the streets of Zzyzx
Then choose Consequences or Truth

KEY, WEST VIRGINIA & KEY WEST, VIRGINIA

Okay, we have word play at work here. We came across this quirky combo and while neither town has much of a tale to tell, we thought the playful punctuation was worthy of a few paragraphs. In case you were reading quickly, so far nothing in this entry has a thing to do with the Florida Keys.

In a bit of a irony, the state of West Virginia has a town called Key, and the state of Virginia has a town called Key West. So placed in the traditional "town, state" order their wording reads the same with the comma in a different position.

For the record, if you were in Key, West Virginia and wanted to get to Key West, Virginia, you'd have a relatively short trip of 112 miles. That being said, once you get to Key West, Virginia if you want to go from one Key West to the other one in Florida, you're looking at a trip of 1,172 miles, about 10 times as long as your previous trip.

ZZYX, CALIFORNIA

This one is fraught with scandal. Quack doctor Curtis Howe Springer was a radio evangelist who tried to convince people he was a legitimate doctor while selling fake medicines on his radio show. The most surprising side to this scurrilous scheme is how long the scam lasted. Here's the timeline.

In 1944 Springer and his wife filed a mining claim for 12,800 acres of public space in southwest California and identified the land claimed as Zzyzx. Who knew it could be so easy? The name was chosen because it would literally be last in any directory listing, strategically supplementing their marketing campaign in which they billed themselves as "the last word in health." For the record the pronunciation of the word is "Zye-zex."

The Springers subsequently enticed tourists and those seeking better health to their "Zzyzx Mineral Springs and Health Resort." Hopefully none of our ardent fans were amongst the schmucks who succumbed to this shtick.

Amazingly, Springer's house of cards was still standing 30 years later. It would be 1974 before things would cave in and when that time came, Springer was exposed on both levels of legal indiscretion.

First, the federal government finally realized Springer didn't have a legitimate claim to the land and evicted him in 1974. Then, perhaps prompted by the American Medical Association's labeling of Springer as the "King of Quacks," he was also called on the carpet for his bogus health claims. Springer's sentence was a surprisingly short 49 days in jail. Seems like a fairly shallow price to pay for illegally using government land to swindle money from people for three decades.

TRUTH OR CONSEQUENCES, NEW MEXICO

This town, which was formerly named Hot Springs, is located in southwest New Mexico, 25 miles from the Mexican border. The population is around 6,500. So how does a town start as Hot Springs and land as Truth or Consequences? Turns out it's all part of the game.

In 1950, Ralph Edwards, the host of the radio quiz show *Truth or Consequences*, announced that he would air the program from the first town that renamed itself after the show. Hot Springs was the first to step up to the line. Officials quickly said "We will!" and the town's name was changed on March 31, 1950, just in time for the live broadcast on April 1.

A permanent bond was formed and Edwards subsequently visited the town during the first weekend of May for the next fifty years. In 1950, regarding the name change from Hot Springs, the mayor tried to counter the suggestion that the town had sold out and abandoned its traditional name in what amounted to a cheesy publicity stunt.

While Hot Springs was appropriate because it described the natural phenomenon for which the town had been named, the mayor expressed the opinion that Truth or Consequences equally defined the town because, "It is the truth that we have the health-giving waters here. The consequences are that people get results." He did not get re-elected.

LAKE CHARGOGGAGOGGMANCHAUGGAGOGGCHAUBUNAGUNGAMAUGG, MASSACHUSETTS

We've been to this lake. Even dipped our toes in the water; a story which we'll get to shortly. This one is unique simply because it has the longest name of any place in all of the United States. Let's cover the numerology first. The name consists of 14 syllables and 45 letters, 15 of which are "g". And it's easier to pronounce than you might think.

The name is a Native American word and the basic translation is, "You fish on your side of the lake, I fish on mine, and nobody fishes in the middle." It's a pretty good size lake covering 1,442 acres and it's located south of Boston, near the Connecticut border, in a town called Webster, Massachusetts. If you want to cop out on tackling the lake's actual name, sometimes people default to "Lake Webster."

You may have thought that we were being facetious with our easy-to-pronounce comment, but we actually weren't. Sure it's a mouthful, but the Indian word is spoken just as the letters would indicate. Here it is phonetically: Lake Char-gogg-a-gogg-man-chau-a-gogg-chau-bun-a-gung-a-maugg.

Our initial take upon first seeing it was that it looked like someone had inadvertently let their hand rest on the keyboard and, as an offshoot, had a range of random letters unknowingly sprawl onto the screen. As unmanageable as the name may be, when the government tried to shorten it in the 1950's that initiative was met with fierce resistance by the townspeople. That attitude is understandable especially if you go there in person.

It is unbelievable how many different times and ways Lake "C" is displayed in the town. It's all over the place. Anytime you're the biggest or best in any regard or category it's a source of pride, and in this case it also contributes to the town's tourism draw in the summer.

There were definitely some "Good Vibrations" in the air when we had our Lake "C" experience. Part of the tourism draw is the Indian Ranch outdoor concert venue which is literally right on the lake. In 2015 we went to a Beach Boys concert at Indian Ranch so that's the backstory on our personal connection to the longest place name in the United States. Next we'll head to Wales for another long one.

LLANFAIRPWLLGWYNGYLLGOGERYCHWYRNDROBWLL LLANTYSILIOGOGOGOCH, WALES

At 58 characters, this tiny Welsh village on the isle of Anglesey has the longest place name in Europe. Translated to English, it's a phrase that describes the town's location: Saint Mary's Church in the hollow of the white hazel near a rapid whirlpool and the Church of St. Tysilio of the red cave.

The town has existed in some form for thousands of years, but in 1880 a publicity-oriented tailor changed its name from Llanfairpwll to its current moniker to bestow upon the train station the honor of having the longest name of any in the U.K. – a move intended to attract tourists. Llanfairpwll is still used when a shorter alternative is desired. We'll finish up this segment on long names by heading down under to New Zealand.

TAUMATAWHAKATANGIHANGAKOAUAUOTAMATEATURIPUKAKAPIKIMAUNGAHORONUKUPOKAIWHENUAKITANATAHU
NEW ZEALAND

Okay, you probably won't be surprised when we tell you this, but you just managed to navigate your way through the longest place name in the world and we're really sure you're going to appreciate our next move. An acceptable truncation is to use the first seven letters of Taumata.

An obvious next question would be, "What the hell does it mean?" Probably equally obvious would be the fact that the English translation will be just as long as the original name which is in the language of the native Maori tribe of New Zealand. What the Aborigine are to Australia, the Maori are to New Zealand.

The translation is "The summit where Tamatea, the man with the big knees, the slider, climber of mountains, the land-swallower who travelled about, played his flute to his loved one." Tamatea was an explorer who was one of the first documented legends of Maori history.

Taumata is a hill in Hawke's Bay, New Zealand, a town which can be located on the southeastern shore of New Zealand's North Island. Since the flute playing from a few millenniums past, not a lot has happened on the hill. They did put up a sign that includes all 85 of the letters which earned Taumata its spot in the *Guinness Book of World Records*.

CHAPTER 10
EXCLAMATIONS! – QUESTIONS? – COMMANDS.

If you'd like to get excited, confused or bossed around, this will be your chapter. We'll cover Charlie Brown's signature exclamation of **Good Grief!** and we will address the classic philosophical questions of **Why** or **WhyNot?** And when it's all said and done you will be directed to **Rest and Be Thankful.**

Why or Why Not, just give me a sec
Pity Me, albatross 'round my neck
Shout "Eek," cry "Good Grief!"
Where to find some relief?
Saint-Louis-Du-Ha!-Ha!, Quebec

SAINT-LOUIS-DU-HA! HA!, QUEBEC, CANADA

Just north of Maine and south of the St. Lawrence Seaway, you'll find Saint-Louis-du-Ha! Ha!, Quebec. This small town was founded in 1860 as a Roman Catholic mission, and today's population rests at around 1,400.

Here's the etymology. The "Saint Louis" part refers to Louis IX (1214-1270) who was the only King of France to also be canonized as a Saint in the Catholic Church. So the dude was a King and a Saint; not a bad resumé.

The "Ha! Ha!" traces back to an archaic French term, "haha," which means an unexpected obstacle or dead end. This reference would be to Lake Témiscouata, which sprung up upon the early French explorers just northeast of the town.

In 2018 the town made it into the *Guinness Book of World Records* as the only geographic location in the world whose name contains two exclamation points. We could find no explanation as to why the exclamation points were added, but we can rule out one possibility. It was not a blatant attempt to get into the record book because the town was named in 1874 and the Guinness Book did not first publish until 1955.

EEK, ALASKA

Located in southwest Alaska, the small town of Eek has a population of about 300. It would be fanciful to think the town might have gotten its name when some early explorers stumbled unexpectedly across a wolf or a bear. In fact the name comes from an Eskimo word meaning "two eyes," although no one seems to know why on earth those Eskimos were inclined to call it Two Eyes in the first place.

GOOD GRIEF, IDAHO

No, this isn't Charlie Brown's hometown, although the phrase was immortalized by America's favorite "blockhead" in the Charles Schulz *Peanuts* comic strips and TV specials. And speaking of vintage TV, it was the 1970's corn pone country music and comedy TV show *Hee Haw* that brought national attention to the town of Good Grief by referring to it on a regular basis as "having a population of three, with two dogs and one old grouch." Good grief!

Here's the lowdown on Good Grief. Around 1900 W.J. Greenway built a compound and named it for his wife Addie. In addition to their living quarters the structure featured a general store and inn. There's a record of the property being sold in 1920 but no record of to whom, and details on the next three decades are sketchy. The only thing our research could turn up from that era was a 1940's picture which showed the building labeled, on different parts of the façade, as a "general store," "café" and "tavern."

Good Grief is only four miles from Canada located in that thin arm of western Idaho that reaches up to the Canadian border. We're not sure how the tavern was established, but we're thinking the zoning laws may have been a little lax in that neck of the woods at that time. The code enforcement boys from Boise probably weren't making a lot of trips north toward the border to monitor the goings on in Good Grief, which wouldn't actually adopt that name until the next decade.

In the mid-1950's Paul Springs bought the establishment as a surprise gift for his wife. He achieved significant success on the "surprise" component of his initiative. When his wife finally saw the place, she summed up her surprise with, you guessed it, a very unenthusiastic, "Good Grief."

The establishment is currently being run by Stanaslov and Svetlana Fetasayev. So if you find yourself in Idaho, on the run for the Canadian border and looking for some relief in Good Grief, stop by and see these S & S kids. Just so you know, the tavern is closed, but you can buy beer, pop and coffee and the café features a nice variety of sandwiches, soups and burgers. And, "Good Grief!", they also sell fishing worms.

WHO'D THOUGHT IT, TEXAS

Who'd Thought It would become a ghost town? At its height of activity, prior to WWII, there were a couple stores in town, but by 1980 everything was closed. We could find no information available on how the town in eastern Texas came to have its quirky name.

WHY, ARIZONA

Located just thirty miles north of the Mexican border, the small town of Why, Arizona, should actually have now changed its name to "Tee." In this case, people originally referred to the place as "Y" because it was at a Y-shaped intersection of two roads.

Then of course the politicians had to get involved. Arizona passed a law stipulating all town names had to have at least three letters. Y ? Who knows. So what did Y do? They changed their name to Why. Why not?

But here's the kicker. A spate of automobile accidents motivated the Arizona Highway Department to reconstruct the intersection. The roads now meet in a T-junction. But at least now you know Why.

WHYNOT, NORTH CAROLINA

This small town in central North Carolina struggled to come up with a name, but when they landed their first post office in the mid-19th century it became a requirement. As the debate raged on, one person would say, "Why not call it this?" Another would say, "Why not call it something else?"

But as is the case with most small towns, there's always a pragmatist in the group. Annoyingly frustrated at one name-committee meeting, our pragmatist finally put an end to the drama, "Why not call it 'Why Not' so we can all go home?" Why Not, indeed? It stuck and over time the two words morphed into one.

PITY ME, ENGLAND

"Pity Me," pleads the signpost welcoming visitors to this northeastern English village. The derivation of the name Pity Me has long been disputed. There are basically three competing theories with one common aspect that is indisputable. Some ugly options are in the mix here.

Theory #1 - When Britain's Saint Cuthbert died, the pall bearers who were carrying his coffin through town for burial accidentally dropped it. In his final miracle, one emanating from the grave, Cuthbert implored the onlooking monks to break into the 51st Psalm which includes the words "Pity me, O God." One expanded version of this account which we read attributed the dropped coffin to a Viking raid. Shit happens, right!?

Theory #2 - The Oxford Dictionary of British Place Names suggests that the moniker is a "whimsical name bestowed in the 19th century on a place considered desolate, exposed or difficult to cultivate."

Theory #3 - These last two both espouse the theory that the name emanates from the influence of the French, imported to Britain, after the Norman invasion of 1066. The village was thought to have been next to a small lake and took its name from "petit mere," the French words meaning "little sea."

Theory #4 - Being a mining area, the name is derived from the expression "pithead mere," an area of boggy waste ground onto which the outwash from minehead pumping engines was discharged.

Of our available options here, the one that is probably the least likely is also probably the most fun. The idea of the dead saint getting pissed off after being dropped by his pall bearers had us almost ready to sing along as well.

REST AND BE THANKFUL MOUNTAIN, SCOTLAND

This mountain is the highest point in the Arrochar Alps in western Scotland. Located less than an hour north of Glasgow, the largest city in Scotland, the mountain is a popular hiking attraction. Rest and Be Thankful describes what you're supposed to do, and then how you're supposed to feel, when you get to the top.

Chapter 11
It's a Numbers Game

It's a numbers game here with these five stories. If you think the scoop on Eighty Four is good, just wait until you get the lowdown on Eighty Eight. And what happens when the good citizens of one Canadian town form a committee to come up with a name for their community and decide to hold a meeting at the local tavern. We'll also sojourn to the South Pacific to visit Thirteen Martyrs in the Philippines and return to America to play ball and hear the story behind the first Major League Baseball player to wear a number higher than 50.

THIRTEEN MARTYRS, PHILIPPINES

The city of Thirteen Martyrs lies in the northwest Philippines with a population of about 150,000. The city, which was originally called Quinta, changed its name after it was the site of an historical event that occurred on September 12, 1896.

At that point in time the Philippines were in the midst of a drive for independence from Spain and inroads were being made. In 1896 thirteen men in this region were heading the organization leading the independence drive in this area of the country. These thirteen men were convicted of rebellion and executed by the Spanish colonial government on the aforementioned date.

In tribute to these men, the city of Quinta was renamed Thirteen Martyrs. Spain wasn't too happy about it, but the natives were going to call their city whatever they pleased and power was beginning to slip away from the Spanish anyway.

So, Filipino independence is knocking at the door, right? Well, not so fast, and this far into it we owe it to you folks to finish that storyline. What went wrong for those independence-loving Filipinos? Ironically, it was the Spanish-American War.

Less than two years after the incident mentioned above, that war was initiated and after Spain was defeated in short order, it was forced to cede all of its colonial territories to the United States, including the Philippines.

With the age of Imperialism still thriving, the U.S. was more powerful than Spain and managed to squelch Filipino independence for another half century. The United States granted independence to the Philippines in 1946, finally fulfilling the work of the Thirteen Martyrs.

EIGHTY FOUR, PENNSYLVANIA

Eighty Four is a small community of 657 people located 25 miles southwest of Pittsburgh and considered to be part of that metropolitan area. The town was originally called Smithville, but Pennsylvania had another Smithville, as well as a New Smithville, so in order to clarify confusion, the Post Office requested a name change.

There are two equally credible theories regarding how the new name was assigned. The date of the change was July 28, 1884 prompting one theory that a very unimaginative postmaster just copied the last two digits of the date and made it the town's name. The other theory floated is that the name comes from the town's place along the 84th mile of the Baltimore and Ohio Railroad line.

A final fun fact of numerology is that the town is the home of the headquarters of the 84 Lumber Company. In this case it's clear that the company named itself after the town. Eighty Four was also the home of the first 84 Lumber store.

EIGHTY EIGHT, KENTUCKY

There are three dates that will always stand out as being the red-letter days in the history of Eighty Eight, Kentucky. Those dates are November 2, 1948, August 8, 1988, and August 8, 2008. The story of the celebrity of those specific days will follow soon. But first let's settle in and set a spell in this quaint country town with a population of about 200.

Eighty Eight is located in rural south central Kentucky, about 10 miles east of Glasgow. Dabnie Nunally, the town's first postmaster, was empowered with coming up with an official name when this country community was bestowed with its own post office in 1848. Nunnally didn't think very highly of his handwriting, and thought that using a number as the town's name would make the legibility on his office work to be less of an issue. To come up with the number, he reached into his pocket and counted his change. He had 88 cents. There you have it... a town was named.

BIG DAY #1 ~ Things were right quiet in Eighty Eight for the next hundred years but on November 2, 1948 the hand of fate caused something unbelievable to happen in town. That day happened to be the first Tuesday, after the first Monday, in November, hence Election Day. It was a presidential election that year with Harry S. Truman facing off against Thomas E. Dewey.

Folks in town were pretty much divided down the middle as to whom they supported in this one. As a matter of fact they were divided exactly down the middle. Now, in and of itself, a 50-50 split of the vote in such a small town would not truly qualify for the aforementioned adjective of "unbelievable." It was the numerology involved that elevated the election to such superlative status.

The final tally in the 1948 election in the town of Eighty Eight was Truman 88, Dewey 88. Honest to God! That trifecta earned the town its first real claim to fame. The 88 to 88 in Eighty Eight enshrined the town in *Ripley's Believe It Or Not* thus immortalizing Eighty Eight forever.

At this point it would make for a probable assumption that this event would qualify as the town's only 15 minutes of fame. That assumption however would be incorrect.

BIG DAY #2 ~ By the second day of January 1988, Postmistress Donnie Sue Bacon knew this year would be different in Eighty Eight. When Mrs. Bacon turned over her outgoing mail to the regional carrier from Bowling Green on January 2, the stack of letters was noticeably heavier than usual. All at once, the Eighty Eight postmark had become a hot item.

By spring she had to retire her old ink pad & stamp and the USPS equipped her with a new self-inking postmark device. People had begun to send mass mailings, such as graduation and wedding announcements, to Eighty Eight so that the recipients would receive their invites with the 1988 "Eighty Eight" postmarks.

From the graduation notices of seniors at the University of Southern California to the invitations for John Denver's wedding, all kinds of people were sending their special mailings through Eighty Eight so they would be delivered bearing the timely postmark. As an out-of-state postal patron told Mrs. Bacon, "This is your year."

And the momentum on this thing was just beginning to grow. In looking at the calendar, the single day upon which the numerology would most awesomely align would be August 8, or 8/8/88. So as the year progressed the notion emerged in town that a local gala would be held. Plans were underway for an event to be billed as "8/8/88 Eve in Eighty Eight." Now we're sure a good time would have been had by all, even if the town had just been left to its own devices. But what happens next is crazy.

Articles about the converging of the year and the place start appearing in newspapers. The idea begins to take root and the media, inevitably, hears about the celebration. As the enthusiasm for the event increases even more through print and electronic media, a national television news program sends in a camera crew, and letters pour in from all over the world. Things are sizzling for Postmistress Bacon! People from Italy to Argentina to Singapore want those letters mailed out of Eighty Eight on 8/8/88.

On August 7, at 8:00 on 8/8/88 Eve in Eighty Eight, CBS comes on the air with live coverage of the event. Highlights include everything from games, to gospel singing, to a parade from one end of town to the other. That parade, which has captured the attention of the country, traverses the trail from the Church of Christ to the Baptist Church, an elaborate route of about half a mile. "I expect the parade will be longer than the route," says Mrs. Rose Mary McPherson, official Eighty Eight parade organizer. She is right.

The grand marshal is 88-year-old Elsie Billingsley, who happens to be the only person in town of precisely that age. Nearly everybody in town is in it, which means the onlookers are all visitors. Turns out the parade route is quite crowded which, given the fact that CBS has been promoting live coverage of the event, is not particularly surprising.

Festivities continue throughout the day on Monday with the culminating event occurring that evening. Eighty Eight would be hosting the wedding at 8:08 of a Wyoming couple who thinks it will be memorable to get married in Eighty Eight that day (the only rub being that if either of them ever forgets the anniversary, it'll be tough to come up with a good excuse). Deb Muhlbeir and Tom Accardo of Casper are attended by seven native Kentucky couples who were married on various August 8's.

BIG DAY #3 ~ So what would be the next big day in Eighty Eight? We'll preface our explanation with the notion that history never repeats itself, but it often rhymes. If you run the numerology through your brain, you might land on the logical premise that it would be August 8, 2008... or 08/08/08. Once again Eighty Eight fever is afoot. There is a sense of déjà vu with most of the same activities recreated from the 1988 event, only everybody is 20 years older. With the summer Olympics ongoing at the time, the competition for media coverage is a bit stiffer, but still everything was great in Eighty Eight on August 8, 2008.

So what's up next for the town? Mark your calendars for August 8, 2088 when it will be 8/8/88 in Eighty Eight again. We hope to see you there.

The 88 cents sealed the fate
Established forever the date
There'd be no debate
The ratings were great
On 8/8/88, Eighty Eight

NINETY SIX, SOUTH CAROLINA

The town of Ninety Six is in the northwest part of South Carolina and has a population of around 2,000. For a small town it has a disproportionate number of historical storylines which we will share with you shortly. We'll start with the multiple theories as to how the town got its name.

Theory #1 - It was 96 miles to the nearest Cherokee settlement of Keowee.

Theory #2 - There were 96 creeks crossing the main road leading from Ninety Six to Lexington, South Carolina. There are only about 70 now but it's known that several have dried up over the years so there's no way to corroborate a creek count going back to the 1700's when the town was named.

Theory #3 - The name is an adaptation of a Welsh expression, *nant-sych*, meaning "dry gulch." The town founder Robert Goudey was Welsh.

One statistic used in basketball is the "triple double" which is when a player achieves double figures in points, rebounds and assists. Since this whole chapter is themed around numerology, let's have some fun with it and award Ninety Six with a "double triple." It has three theories as to the origin of the name and three substantial historical storylines. Let's do those next.

History #1 - The first land battle of the Revolutionary War, south of New England, was fought in Ninety Six from November 19-21, 1775. Note that this date actually precedes the Declaration of Independence. This contributes to the fact that the town has been designated as an official National Historic Site. For more on this, see below.

History #2 - Here's one with a particular appeal for those Jewish readers in our audience. Before it became Ninety Six the town was initially known as "Jews Land" because some prominent Jewish families from London bought extensive property there, intending to help some poor Jewish families relocate from London to the New World.

On August 1, 1776, less than a month after the Declaration of Independence, American militia forces confronted the British here in the Battle of Twelve Mile Creek. Francis Salvador, a Jewish immigrant from London, was one of the casualties. He was the first Jew to be killed fighting for the Americans in the Revolutionary War.

Since the late 20th century, the National Park Service has operated the Ninety Six National Historic Site at the location of the original settlement and fort where Francis Salvador gave his life.

History #3 ~ Ninety Six was the home of a significant Major League Baseball player. From 1942-1950, Bill Voiselle was a pitcher for the New York Giants, Boston Braves and Chicago Cubs. In 1944 he was named to the National League All-Star team, led the league in strike outs, and won the *Sporting News* award for Pitcher of the Year.

During that era, baseball players traditionally wore low numbers on their uniforms and Voiselle brought a unique change to Major League Baseball. In a gesture to honor his home town, Voiselle petitioned the Commissioner of Major League Baseball to become the first player to ever wear a number beginning with a number higher than the 40's.

And not just above the 40's. Voiselle gained approval for the numerical exception and took the field wearing number 96 during his major league baseball career. If you think this story is good you should definitely follow up on the reciprocal numerical story, the one on Sixty Nine, which appeared in our second book, *Tit For Tat Exchanges ~ Tim & Deb's Greatest Hits*.

WONOWON, BRITISH COLUMBIA

Just to clarify why this is coming up in the numbers chapter, the pronunciation of the town is "one-oh-one." It was originally called "Blueberry," which makes "Wonowon" seem like it's one step down, doesn't it? Why give up the sweet fruit for the mundane numbers? Here's the scoop, and we're not talking blueberry ice cream.

In an agricultural fun fact we hope most of you have not taken the time to research, turns out that of all the provinces in Canada, British Columbia produces 96% of the blueberries grown. With that fact in hand, it's perhaps not surprising that more than one community in the province had named itself "Blueberry."

When the Canadian postal system reached the level of sophistication where it was starting to sort out these types of problems, protocol procedures required that because this Blueberry was the smaller of the two Blueberries it would have to change its name.

So what happens next? This news apparently gives Blueberry the blues. During a town tavern "new-name" meeting, the committee charged with the change walks down to the local north/south expressway and notices that they are located at mile marker #101 on Highway 97, the Alaska Highway which runs from Spokane to Juneau.

We truly would love to have the minutes to this meeting, as well as a printout of the bar tab. Somehow sobriety seems to be setting like the sun simultaneously with someone spotting the #101 mile marker. One guy points at the sign and says, "I'd give my right arm to be ambidextrous."

The suggestion is sailed, "Let's call the town 101, head back to the bar and I'll buy the next round of drinks." Clearly opting for the quirky-over-creative approach, the committee decides to opt for the new name of 101.

As the alcoholic frenzy of frivolity ensues during the final round of drinks, the committee coalesces to the acceptance of the fact that "101" probably wasn't the most enlightened name they might have come up with. So with the increased flow of alcohol with this group simultaneously overlapping with the decreased flow in brainwave activity, the following compromise is reached… we've locked our drunken asses into 101 but, we'll spell it out. While we're not sure how strictly Robert's Rules of Order were enforced at this point, the group decision could be summed up as follows, "Wonowon it was." Wonderful.

When the meeting was all said and done
Time does fly when you're just having rum
Or was it the wine?
When they did see the sign
Blueberry became Wonowon

Chapter 12
NOT FOR NOTHING

If this chapter didn't exist, it would be a loss because there are some good stories here. Actually you will go **Nowhere** with **No Place** and **No Name**. What's the **Point? No Point.**

Let's put somebody's nose out of joint
Kings of nothingness we will anoint
There's no prizes to claim
No Place or No Name
Going Nowhere but to Point No Point

NO NAME, COLORADO

Located in the northwest quadrant of the state is the small town of No Name, Colorado, population 123. The community received its name after Interstate 70 was constructed in 1956. Shortly after its completion, the Colorado Department of Transportation set out to establish signage. The Department of Transportation official who was labeling the exit signs was working from a map that had Exit 118 leading to Pataskala and Exit 120 going to Glenwood Springs.

On his map there were no municipalities identified between those two towns but there was one exit in between. So the DOT official labeled Exit 119 as "No Name." It stuck. While you might think that the folks in the area of Exit 119 would have reacted negatively to the anonymity of the name, or lack thereof, exactly the opposite came to be true. State officials once tried to rename the area, but the locals said "No Way."

The area has embraced the moniker to the point that its applications have been on the rise over the past three decades. There is now a No Name Creek and No Name Canyon. The No Name Tunnel of I-70 is also nearby. Its unique name even landed the town in a movie. The exit sign for No Name is shown in the 1971 film *Vanishing Point* starring Barry Newman.

NO PLACE, DURHAM, ENGLAND

No Place is actually some place. It's a small village located in northeast England. The origins of the village's unusual name are uncertain; with three competing theories.

Theory #1 - The name of the village was a shortening of "North Place."

Theory #2 - The four original houses of the village stood on a boundary between two parishes, neither of which would accept the village.

Theory #3 - It was a tax evasion scam whereby when asked by the tax collector where they were from, locals could truthfully reply, "No Place."

The backstory on the history of the area can be a little confusing and we're going to try to do a better job of explaining this to you than any of our research sources did when it was first explained to us. Originally No Place consisted of just four houses (the houses alluded to in #2 above). In 1937, residents of a larger community of houses to the north, known as Co-operative Villas, bought and demolished the four houses in No Place and usurped the town's name for their own village.

In 1983 a movement took hold whereby some of the villagers wanted to revert from "No Name" to their original "Co-operative Villas." Community sentiment on the whole however strongly favored No Name which was officially retained. In deference to those who favored it, "Co-operative Villas" was added to some of the signage.

NOWHERE, OKLAHOMA

If you'd ever like to find yourself in the middle of nowhere, that can literally happen for you in southwest Oklahoma. Nowhere is sparsely populated, but its location on State Highway 146 leading to Fort Cobb State Park generates enough through traffic to sustain the Nowhere General Store which is also a gas station and bait house for folks heading to the park to do some fishing.

The Nowhere General Store is owned by Jerry Howell and we gave him a call to garner some information about this locale. When we talked to Jerry he'd been going nowhere, so to speak, for 30 years. We asked him about how the town got its name and he told us that it used to be owned by a guy named Benny Shanks who called the place Benny's Boat House.

A couple from California bought the boat house and when the wife saw what the husband had gotten her into she complained, "You've brought me out to nowhere and I don't like it one bit." Playing upon that, they adopted "Nowhere" as the name of the general store and eventually that name came to be used as the moniker to identify the crossroads community.

We asked Jerry what the population of Nowhere was and it didn't take him long to do the math. "It's myself, my daughter and my grandson. Population 3."

POINT NO POINT, WASHINGTON

This geological area on the northeast point of the Kitsap Peninsula was named in 1841 by Commander Charles Wilkes, who led the U.S. Exploring Expedition of Puget Sound, which was the first major voyage of exploration sponsored by the U.S. government. Wilkes gave the point its name because it appeared much less of a promontory at close range than it did from out at sea. There is another "Point No Point" located on the Hudson River and that may have been the impetus for Wilkes reusing the name for this spot in Washington.

For what it's worth, no racial group seemed to be in love with the place when it came to bestowing names. The local Native Americans called the area *Hahd-skus*, or long nose. Looking to close on a positive note, we'll share the fact that Point No Point is a paradise of natural habitat. It is one of the most noted bird-watching destinations in the country.

Chapter 13
DON'T BE SO NEGATIVE

This chapter is the ultimate downer. You think you've got it bad? How would you like being dumped on **Dumb Women's Lane**, left with **Little Hope** in **Idiotville**? Or you could be stranded at **Misery Bay** in the **Disappointment Islands** reliving the **Useless Loop** of **Taylor's Mistake** and feeling **Very Stupid** that you're such a **Tightwad**. If you survive all this, we'll try to cheer you up in the next chapter.

TAYLOR'S MISTAKE, NEW ZEALAND

Most cities wouldn't want to be known as a "mistake," but this quaint, coastal town on the South Island of New Zealand actually has three overlapping theories contributing to its maritime mishap moniker. So who is this Taylor dude and what was his mistake?

The answer to that question actually takes on an air of Twilight Zone eeriness. Within a span of just a dozen years in the mid-19th century there were three different maritime mishaps, all of which involved a man named Taylor! How weird is that? Here's the rundown of what happened at the locale that was originally known as Vincent's Bay.

Incident #1 - In 1853 Captain Underwood of the ship Gwalior threw himself overboard in the bay. Chief Officer Taylor took over and his failure to save the captain qualified as the first Taylor mistake.

Incident #2 - In 1858 a Captain Taylor mistook the bay's identity and beached his ship the Volga.

Incident #3 - In 1864 yet another Captain Taylor made yet another similar mistake and ran his ship Catherine aground at the bay.

Our conclusion would be that if you have three different Taylors screw things up in your poor town, then Taylor's Mistake is a name you are probably destined to own.

We're going to conclude with yet another Taylor's Mistake story which we'll call "Howard's Mistake" or "Can Somebody Lend Me a Hand?" On December 16, 1885 at Taylor's Mistake, a bay already shrouded in mystery and maritime drama, a hand was found by two men fishing off the rocks.

Identified by a ring still on it, the hand was claimed by a Mrs. Sarah Howard as being that of her husband. Mr. Arthur Howard's clothing had been found on the beach earlier that year on the 11th of October. Mr. Howard had $3,000 in life insurance, a considerable amount of money for that time which would equate to about $80,000 today.

The sum Mrs. Howard stood to gain from her husband's demise, combined with the fact that the fishermen seemed a bit fishy, served to raise police suspicions. This led to the two fishermen and Mrs. Howard being arrested for conspiracy to defraud an insurance company. Mr. Howard was later tracked down at a YMCA picnic (both hands intact) and was also arrested.

The hand was later identified as that of a woman, but despite the exhumation of several graves in an attempt to discover the hand's owner, to this day the identity of the woman is not known. So what do we take away from all this? If you are participating in an insurance fraud where your alleged death is a key component of the scurrilous scam, partying down at the local YMCA picnic should probably drop way down on your "to do" list.

VERY STUPID, FRANCE

Believe it or not, there is actually an Association of French Villages with Funny Names. Better yet, they have an annual convention. In a move that seems way overdue, at their most recent convention the association accepted Very Stupid into its ranks. Very Stupid is a town of about a hundred people located in northeast France.

Georges Leherle, the mayor of Very Stupid was very proud to have the town inducted as the 39th member of the group. "I'm always happy to tell people where I live, I can't deny it," he said. "And you know," Leherle added, "despite the name of our town, we're no stupider than anyone else."

IDIOTVILLE, OREGON

Idiotville is a ghost town and former logging community northwest of Portland. Most of its former residents worked at a nearby logging camp called Ryan's Camp. Since the spot was so remote, it was said that only an idiot would work there, so the camp was popularly known as Idiotville.

The name was eventually applied to the nearby stream and Idiotville as well as Idiot Creek were officially applied to community maps. Only an idiot would see it any differently.

TIGHTWAD, MISSOURI

This small western Missouri village has just 64 people, but it does have one great story. As is often the case, these small town stories about how name changes came about long ago are often passed down in various versions. Here's our compilation on this one.

Tightwad was originally called Edgewood, in a name that described the town's location. This one's pretty simple; it was located at the edge of the woods. In the town there was a penny-pinching farmer who we'll cast as Edgewood's Ebenezer Scrooge in this unscrupulous 19th century saga.

Back in those days, in any small town, the postmaster and the mail delivery man would have been the same person. Let's call him Bob for the sake of the story. On one late summer day in 1843, Bob, who lives in the neighboring town of Leesville, is delivering mail to Edgewood Ebenezer who has some produce for sale including one mouthwatering watermelon.

Bob thinks the melon would make a great late summer treat for his family, agrees to purchase the item, and Ebenezer promises he can pick it up on his way home from work. Upon completing his rounds, Bob heads home by the Ebenezer farm to pick up his melon. Bob arrives at the farm only to find out that the melon has been absconded, sold to a customer who had offered 10¢ more than he had.

As the postmaster angrily leaves, he shouts "Tightwad!" at the farmer and, as we all know, some folks take their watermelons more seriously than others. In those early days, postmasters could freely submit place-name suggestions to the USPS. As Edgewood finds out, Hell hath no fury like that of a postmaster scorned.

Following the criteria in place at the time, that any name change requests must be short, easy to read and write, and not the same as any existing places in the state, the pissed off postmaster facilitates the processing of the paperwork that changes the name of the town's post office, and hence the town, from Edgewood to Tightwad.

Perhaps ironically, the citizens came to embrace the name. Nowadays you can take a summer stroll on Stingy Street and make your way to Miser Street. There's even a Tightwad Bank. If you make a withdrawal there, be sure to take out that extra dime so you'll be able to score the best watermelon in Tightwad.

USELESS LOOP, AUSTRALIA

Located on the eastern shore of Australia, Useless Loop is a closed company town, a phrase we will explain next. The entire town consists of the salt mining operation of Shark Bay Salt Party Limited, its 70 employees and their families. So you can extrapolate the overall population from there. There's probably a few hundred people in the Loop.

Here's the storyline on the unusual name. In 1801 when French explorer Henri-Louis de Freycinet was exploring Australia he came across the bay here which he perceived to be blocked by a sandbar and hence useless for ships. He turned out to be incorrect about the sandbar, but before he found that out he had labeled the body of water Useless Harbor. Over time that morphed into Useless Loop.

In 1962 vast salt mines were discovered which led to the formation of the Shark Bay Company. This mining town actually produces the purest form of salt in the world today, so as it turned out, Useless Loop was far from useless.

MISERY BAY, MICHIGAN

Misery Bay is located at the mouth of Misery River, which at least is logical. It is said that the river and bay got the name "Misery" because of a bloody battle between two bands of Indians, after which the river ran red.

Playing upon the Native American connection, Misery Bay is not too far away from Eastern Michigan University which is one of only five colleges in the United States that managed to meet the difficult NCAA standards required to keep traditional Native American nicknames. In achieving this status, the Eastern Michigan Chippewas join the Florida State Seminoles, Utah Utes, Catawba Indians, and Mississippi College Choctaws.

PECULIAR, MISSOURI

Coming up with an acceptable town name proved frustrating in one Missouri town in the 1800's. Townspeople came up with three different names and the local postmaster submitted them, but all were rejected because they were already in use. He subsequently sent a letter to the U.S. Postmaster General saying, "We don't care what name you give us so long as it's sort of peculiar."

Probably with tongue in cheek, the postmaster general wrote a long and courteous reply. He said he had given their predicament grave consideration. "My conclusion," he wrote, "is that in all the land it would be difficult to imagine a more distinctive, a more peculiar name than Peculiar." That proclamation came down on June 22, 1868 and things have remained Peculiar there ever since.

Peculiar is located in western Missouri about 30 miles south of Kansas City and the small city boasts a population of just over 4,000.

Useless Loop's at the end of its rope
Misery Bay's got a slippery slope
Strange but it's true
There's Peculiar, Mizzou
Worst of all we still have Little Hope

LITTLE HOPE, TEXAS

This one's mostly about the church whence the community acquired its name. The town first appeared on maps in the 1850's and an 1857 school record identifies the only teacher as being 15-year-old Emily Smith. She may have been young but at least she never had to be concerned with problems regarding class size. The population of Little Hope was indicated as being 13.

By 1881 the community had grown and the Missionary Baptist Church was organized and built a house of worship. The settlers here were apparently not very optimistic about the community's future. They named the church Little Hope expressing their opinion regarding the town's chances for survival. The church name was eventually adopted by the community.

But pessimism be damned, the church survived. That being said, there were some quirky survival skills that contributed to the process; the church had to rent out and share their building with some other organizations in order to stay afloat.

For example, we're not sure what the mission statement was for the "Woodmen of the World" but they sound like a fun group of guys. Despite the possibility of the sexual double entendre implied by their name, we're thinking these men were on the up and up (no pun intended) because they were allowed to have their meetings in the church building from 1900–1922.

Little Hope never had a post office and the last census figures date to the late thirties when the population was down to a mere 10 people. But while the people left, the church managed to survive even though we're sure they were lonelier after the loss of the Woodmen of the World.

Throughout the 1960's, many houses in the area were abandoned, while the congregation of the church increased to over 100. The church inherited a bell from the school at nearby Common Ridge, and erected a belfry to house it. Little Hope Church held a special service to acknowledge the installation of its historical marker in 1985.

DISAPPOINTMENT ISLANDS, FRENCH POLYNESIA

In 1765, Lord Byron's grandfather John Byron had sailed around the tip of South America headed toward India when he chanced upon a tiny island in the distance. To him and his scurvy-ridden crew, it looked like paradise, but he soon realized the high surf and coral reefs prevented safe anchorage.

That, in addition to the spear-wielding natives stationed along the shore, dashed their hopes so severely that Byron named the island (and its nearby sister landmass) the Islands of Disappointment. This may have shielded the islands from centuries of follow-up explorers, but it also literally gives them a bad name.

DUMB WOMAN'S LANE, SUSSEX, ENGLAND

Subtlety is not this Sussex street's strong point, that's for sure. There are a couple of theories floating around about the origins of this idyllic country lane's unfortunate name. And in both of these theories the word "dumb" refers to a lack of speech versus a lack of intelligence.

Theory #1 ~ The first involves a mute woman who used to live there, dispensing herbal remedies to the locals – a vocation that was significant enough that the lane be renamed in her honor.

Theory #2 ~ The second, and more macabre version, tells the tale of a poor woman who witnessed contraband goods being hidden in the area. For centuries, the road was a thoroughfare for smugglers, who brought in lace, brandy and tobacco from France. When the poor woman threatened to expose the operation, the smugglers made a preemptive strike and cut her tongue off to keep her quiet!

You know what they say; a pirate's gotta do, what a pirate's gotta do.

CHAPTER 14
FROM MEDIOCRE TO BORING

Don't be **Lost** or **Uncertain**; this chapter is more than just **Okay**. We will tell you the true story of how three towns in three different countries banded together in a unique "League of Extraordinary Places." Rather than being despondent over their uninspired town names, the communities of **Boring**, Oregon; **Dull**, Scotland; and **Bland**, Australia bonded together in a "Trinity of Tedium" and managed to turn all three communities into tourist destinations, a concept that isn't very Boring at all.

> *Dull, Boring and Bland were all hurtin'*
> *For tourism to raise the curtain*
> *What the hell could we say*
> *Were they Lost or Okay?*
> *Of the answer we feel quite Uncertain*

BORING, OREGON

Located about 12 miles southeast of Portland; Boring, Oregon boasts a population of about 8,000. While this town did not land on the most exciting name, the locals do have a great sense of humor and have made the best of it. Here is a testimonial to that. Boring, Oregon has officially affiliated itself as a sister city with Dull, Scotland and Bland, Australia.

Boring took its name from early settler William Harrison Boring, a Civil War veteran who began farming there in 1874, and subsequently donated land for the community's first schoolhouse to be built. William Boring lived to the ripe old age of 91 and was buried with his wife Sarah in the local cemetery in 1932.

So, the name isn't meant to describe the goings-on in the town. William Boring's great-grandson Bob still lives in the area and says that despite the name, "There's always something going on around here." The name "Boring" is embraced by locals, and found in many local business names, resulting in many signs there that take on a double meaning like the Boring Movie Theater, Boring Comedy Club and

Boring High School. The town's motto is "Boring – The most exciting place to live."

If you find yourself in Boring, asking yourself the question, "What would those interesting Smiths suggest we do?", here's our recommendation. Grab a bite to eat at The Not So Boring Bar & Grill on SE Wally Rd. where the menu extends far beyond typical pub fare. The fish tacos featuring cod get particular standout reviews, and once you're done eating, a game of darts or pool awaits you.

After you've partied in Boring you'll be ready to visit the town's two sister cities, Dull and Bland.

DULL, SCOTLAND

Dull, Bland and Boring might sound like a bad TripAdvisor review, but this Scottish village, along with its Australian and American counterparts, are using the unexciting names to their advantage. We just covered Boring, so please allow us to introduce you to Dull, and then we'll talk about how the two towns "twinned" each other. Dull is a small town located 75 miles north of Glasgow and home to around 100 people. Despite its name, this Highlands region is home to some of Scotland's most breath-taking scenery.

The collaboration between Boring and Dull was initiated in July of 2012 when Dull resident Elizabeth Leighton happened to bicycle through Boring while vacationing in the U.S. The idea occurred to her that Boring and Dull could be bound and determined to form a mutually symbiotic relationship.

By the end of the year the two towns "twinned" one another cementing an official relationship. Signage went up in each town proclaiming the partnership and helping to bolster a burst of tourism in each location.

"Many of the people in Dull have been across the pond to Oregon and visited folks in Boring," said Dull councilman Ian Campbell, "and people from Boring regularly turn up in our village and are pleased to be here. You get a constant procession of people stopping with cars to get their photographs taken in front of the 'Dull and Boring' signs. It's a bit like visiting a sight that you see on the telly."

"Dull has helped put Boring on our map," said Campbell, "and I suspect maybe in certain ways we've helped put Dull on some other maps as well." You could say the pairing has made Boring a little more interesting," said Boring politician Bill Kennemer, "people are starting to hear about Boring and they come and stop." And just when you're thinking things couldn't get any more interesting ...

BLAND, NEW SOUTH WALES, AUSTRALIA

Boring and Dull, meet Bland. Constantly having to put up with the same old jokes and jabs about their dreary names, the marriage became a threesome in 2017 when the towns officially adopted a three-way embrace of their unusual identities.

Speaking at the time, Shire of Bland Mayor Neil Pokoney said, "Dull and Boring basically enjoy an increase in tourism through the connection. We heard about it and thought it would be even better if it became Bland, Dull and Boring. It's good for us to be able to take a light-hearted look at names that many would seem to be a weight around our necks."

In looking for an umbrella moniker to spread over the triumvirate of towns, two emerged as mutual favorites so they were both adopted. The "League of Extraordinary Places" can be used to describe Bland, Dull and Boring as can the "Trinity of Tedium."

Dennis Melloy, Provost of Bland, told BBC Radio Scotland, "These pairings – Dull, Boring and Bland – are just wonderful for tourism and the economy but I think the most important part is the forging of links and the joining of hands across the seas." Melloy went on to indicate that membership in the club may not be confined, going on to add, "We've found Ordinary and Dreary, both in America, and I think they could soon be part of it all."

LOST, ABERDINESHIRE, SCOTLAND

This hamlet in western Scotland has a population of 24 and a problem with people wanting to steal the town's signs. As a result, the Aberdeenshire Council tried to change its name to *Lost Farm*; however, in the face of strong local opposition, the hamlet's traditional name was soon reinstated.

The name comes from the Gaelic word for inn. Today the hamlet has a few houses, a war memorial and a farm. So all is not lost.

OKAY, OKLAHOMA

Permanently muddled in mediocrity, Okay is a small village with 620 people located in the northeast corner of Oklahoma about 50 miles east of Tulsa. In the early 1900's the town had the postal designation of North Muskogee but the townsfolk were clamoring for something with more of their own identity.

In 1919 they adopted Okay as a tribute to the O.K. 3-Ton Truck and Trailer manufactured there by the Oklahoma Auto Manufacturing Company. It's the only example in the country where if you pronounce the town, followed by the two-letter postal code, you are precisely repeating yourself. Letters to this location are addressed to Okay, OK.

UNCERTAIN, TEXAS

Located on the shores of beautiful Caddo Lake, you can find Uncertain in eastern Texas, near the border with Louisiana. The population is certainly decreasing. As of the 2000 census it stood at 150; in 2010, it had decreased to 94; and the 2018 figure came in at 59. There are two competing theories as to how the town got its quirky name.

Theory #1 - The town "derives its name from surveyors who were attempting to delineate the border between Texas and Louisiana and discovered that they were 'uncertain' as to which side of the line they were on as they began surveying that particular part of Caddo Lake."

Theory #2 - The name came from the original application for township where the name for it had not been decided. Therefore, when the original residents filled out the application they put "Uncertain" in the blank for the name. When the township was officially established, it then became "Uncertain."

Chapter 15
OUR BODY OF WORK

We hope you like our body of work here. We're going to have you covered inside and out on this one. We'll delve to the core and get the story on **My Large Intestine** which can be found in Texas and we'll head east to Alabama where we'll get the itch for **Scratch Ankle**.

We'll find out why in the world a place would come to be known as **Port Circumcision**, but we're going to save the real kicker for last. How do you think the town of **Leg-In-Boot** got its name? We'll save the details for later, but know this much, we feel like we're literally going to break a leg with this chapter.

MY LARGE INTESTINE, TEXAS

If you think the name of this place is sad, the picture will truly bring you to tears. Their Facebook page shows a short hundred-foot long dilapidated stretch of commercial buildings with about six on each side of the road. The view in the picture is shot directly down the center line of the street and there is literally not a car or person in view and every building visible is boarded up and signless.

There is an online population count of 143. Based upon the picture, all of the My Large Intestinites currently do their shopping out of town. It was named by its founder, the almost as impressively named Philo Bumbaugh. Mr Bumbaugh's plan was to put the town on the map, but he didn't succeed in the literal sense as no map-makers have yet included it. The aforementioned Facebook page features a map of Texas with an arrow pointing at My Large Intestine with the question, "Why aren't we here?"

To explain where "here" would be for My Large Intestine we're going to get some help from Hollywood. The legendary James Dean only starred in three movies before his tragic death in 1955 when his Jaguar Spyder collided head-on with another vehicle. Employing the title of one of those three films, *East of Eden*, My Large Intestine is located in central Texas about 5 miles east of Eden.

Just to end on a positive spin, the abandoned picture of My Large Intestine which we described above is not totally lifeless. Upon close inspection an armadillo can be seen crossing the street at the bottom.

BIG ARM, MONTANA

This town got its name from the fact that it is located on the Big Arm Bay of the nearby Flathead Lake, a popular destination for fishing. While "Big Arm" is the name for the town on one side of the lake, on the other side is the equally fun Elmo, Montana.

As of 2020 the population was 201 up from the 177 indicated in the 2010 census. While the population is fairly small, it seems like the houses must be fairly large. The average cost of buying new digs in Big Arm is $350,000. That's a pretty healthy investment to live in the-middle-of-nowhere, Montana.

PORT CIRCUMCISION, ANTARCTICA

Port Circumcision is a cove indenting the southeast side of Petermann Island in Antarctica. This would be amongst the chain of islands that reaches up toward the southern tip of South America. It was first discovered by the French Antarctic Expedition of 1908-1910 which was led by Captain Jean-Baptiste Charcot.

The discovery was made on January 1, 1909 which, in the Roman Catholic calendar, is the date of the Feast of the Circumcision of Christ. That was the basis for the name and the cove served as a base for the French during the 1909 winter season.

We're hoping this one doesn't leave you feeling a little bit empty like it did us. Why do we say that? Well, for all these years we've wasted January 1st watching football and hailing the Happy New Year never knowing we could have been celebrating the Feast of the Circumcision of Christ. Next year we're going to be ready.

SCRATCH ANKLE, ALABAMA

This small town of about 200 people is located in southern Alabama about 80 miles southwest of Montgomery and 12 miles from Monroeville, which was the small hometown of famous authors Truman

Capote (*In Cold Blood*) and Harper Lee (*To Kill a Mockingbird*), as we mentioned in Chapter 2.

The long-story-short of it is that the town is apparently infested with insects. When visitors to town noticed the natives frequently scratching their ankles they asked why and the consensus was insect bites. The identification of the offending bugs ranged from mosquitoes to fleas to black gnats. Scratch Ankle is apparently a menagerie of biting insects.

Whatever the culprits are, we'll just leave you with two bits of advice. If you ever visit Scratch Ankle, bring your Off! insect repellant and keep your pant legs rolled down.

LEG-IN-BOOT SQUARE, VANCOUVER, BRITISH COLUMBIA, CANADA

Here's a name certain to raise some eyebrows. Or give people cause to seek out their marching orders, half of them anyway. This urban square in Canada has two unique stories to share with plot lines separated by about 130 years.

Sometimes an 800-pound gorilla is really an 800-pound gorilla. As this storyline goes, in 1887 a full half of a human leg washed up on the shores of nearby False Creek, still wearing its boot. Baffled by the severed extremity, the constables seemingly decided that rather than pounding the pavement trying to identify its owner, they would simply spear the leg on a spike and leave it outside the precinct office in case the owner came by looking for it.

Passersby were too stunned to look and too stunned to leave. Perhaps not surprisingly, the lost leg went unclaimed and after two weeks was assumedly thrown out or simply given to a stray dog in keeping with the apparent police disinterest in expending any man hours on the case.

The police station that once sat in the area is long since gone, and now the spot where the washed-up appendage morbidly flew like a meaty flag is now a cobblestoned shopping plaza. Still no word on the leg's owner.

> *It washed up on the shore over there*
> *Just one leg in a boot solitaire*
> *What the hell do we do?*
> *We just feel inclined to*
> *Stick the leg on a stake in the square*

So, what was once the site of an 1800's atrocity is now an attractive city square. Perhaps in an effort to atone for the malfeasances of the past, British Columbians decided that Leg-in-Boot Square was worthy of a modern-day upgrade.

In July of 2018, as part of the Vancouver Biennale, the square was blessed with an imposing sculpture bearing a weighty name reflective of the sculpture itself. It's called *Acoustic Anvil: A Small Weight to Forge The Sea*, sculpted by Maskull Lasserre. The huge monument dwarfs the people who come to see it, measuring in at a colossal 13 by 25 by 9 feet.

And it's not just a big hunk of metal. In the middle of the piece is a sound-hole. It's based on the principle of the center hole of a violin or a cello. And from inside this channel comes the sound of the ocean. In addition to its musical ability it has solar panels and hidden electronics.

Acoustic Anvil sits on its feet like an ancient, rusting artifact left by giants. Solid and mostly red with streaks of brown and orange, it stretches from a ship-like prow on one side to a blunt, stubby end on the other.

Why an anvil? Acoustic Anvil is an enlarged version of the anvil used for hundreds of years by blacksmiths in the area to work metal. It honors False Creek's history as the city's first industrial center where several sawmills and other businesses were located.

Just to bring history home, and complete the circle of life, we've sent the following suggestion to Vancouver. How about enhancing the anvil imagery by adding a giant sculpture of a blacksmith wielding his hammer… missing one leg.

Chapter 16
Pain in the Ass

This chapter finds us in arrears, so to speak. Lots of potential for segues in this chapter. How better to deal with a **Scratchy Bottom** than to **Scratch My Arse**? We have a **Backside** story or two that don't sound very attractive. Would you rather your date hail from **Six Mile Bottom** or **Big Butt Mountain**? It's a **Ragged Ass Road** to either of those places. But we promise to leave you on a very positive note. We will close the chapter with the arousing story of a truly **Superior Bottom**.

BACKSIDE, SCOTLAND

Located in the council area of Aberdeenshire, Backside is surprisingly beautiful. Too bad it has such an unfortunate name. Perpetuating that quirky-name theme, we could add that the creek that flows through town is called Tammie's Burn. It's the dreaded double curse. Your town makes you sound like an ass and your only body of water sounds like a bad nickname for a urinary tract infection.

SCRATCHY BOTTOM, ENGLAND

Scratchy Bottom is a valley located between two cliffs in southwest England on the shores of the English Channel. The name basically refers to the rough terrain at the bottom of the valley.

Most obscure locations like this would never achieve their 15 minutes of fame. Scratchy Bottom actually has two somewhat significant moments in the limelight. The opening scene of the 1967 film *Far from the Maddening Crowd* was shot here. In that scene Gabriel Oak's sheep are driven over a cliff by his sheepdog.

Scratchy Bottom's second highlight came in 2012 when it came in second in a poll of "Britain's Worst Place Names" conducted by the genealogy website *Find My Past*. Just to put the competition in perspective we'll let you know the one Scratchy Bottom lost to and the one it just beat out. Coming in third in the poll was Brokenwind, Scotland and the place achieving the distinction of having Britain's worst place name was... drum roll... Shitterton.

SIX MILE BOTTOM, ENGLAND

While we've had some bountiful butt references in our book, this one probably wins the award for the biggest butt of all. Located in eastern England, Six Mile Bottom is a small village of just 82 people.

Here's the explanation for the name. In Britain the word "bottom" is somewhat frequently used to refer to a valley. This village is located in a valley which is six miles from the Newmarket Racecourse, a local landmark. So don't be fooled by the name; the locals are said to have butts of just average size.

BIG BUTT MOUNTAIN, NORTH CAROLINA

Big Butt is a summit inside the Great Smoky Mountains National Park in western North Carolina. The mountain has an elevation of about 6,000 feet. Probably not a lot of mystery to the backstory on this one. The mountain has double peaks, both of which are rounded, giving the general appearance of a big butt.

KIESTER, MINNESOTA

If you're looking for a town that has been the butt of many jokes, please call Kiester to the top of your list. It's located in southern Minnesota only a few miles from the Iowa border, and referring next to population, as we often do, there are 501 kiesters in Kiester.

After a century of sitting on their asses, good-naturedly taking ribbings about the town name, in 2016 Kiester cashed in while laughing their asses off all the way to the bank. That was the year when the hemorrhoid medication Preparation H offered them big bucks to use their town as the backdrop for a commercial.

And it turned out to be one kick-ass commercial. You absolutely will not believe what they managed to shove into one 15-second spot. It starts out with one smokin' hot chick posed at the "Welcome to Kiester" sign, her ass firmly planted on a bicycle seat.

The hot chick's opening line of the commercial is, "You wouldn't believe what's in this Kiester." In the following 15 seconds the girl verbally salutes Kiester's Farmer's Market, Marching Band, and Fire Department.

If you can take your eyes off her ass long enough to notice, the background features the Kiester Market, school, theatre and if by this point you're looking for something to blow your snow, Kiester Implement lies right ahead.

> *See the girl on the bike and at least your*
> *Certainly pleased she's surceased her*
> *Attempts to play coy then*
> *She'll be your sex toy when*
> *She wants you to check out her Kiester*

ANUS, FRANCE

If you were French and in your capital city of Paris, would you find it a source of comfort or concern that your Anus was just over a hundred miles away? It's out in the back end of the Province of Burgundy. And here you thought you couldn't live without it.

So what's up with the end story on Anus? And if you find yourself in France, is it worth a visit? The answers to these two questions would be… not much actually and probably not. After you've snapped that funny picture of yourself by the "Welcome to Anus" sign, you've pretty much exhausted the village's "things to do in Anus" list.

There is one commercial entity in town which is the Anus Bread and Breakfast. It is difficult to gauge the quality of this establishment because the online reviews consist primarily of prankish puns which we'll leave to your imagination.

SCRATCH MY ARSE ROCK, COOK ISLANDS

Scratch My Arse Rock is a coral reef that became a popular fishing location off the coast of Palmerston Island, which is one of the islands comprising the nation of the Cook Islands. The area is noted for its abundance of parrotfish.

According to legend, one 19th century fisherman sitting on a rock was asked what he was going to do until the fish started biting. His facetious response was, "I'm going to just sit here and scratch my arse." We love a man with a plan. It stuck.

RAGGED ASS ROAD, YELLOWKNIFE, NORTHWEST TERRITORIES, CANADA

The best things in life are worth fighting for, right? While the success wasn't achieved without controversy, by the time the community of Yellowknife in the Northwest Territories of Canada officially held its festivities for the 50th Anniversary of Ragged Ass Road in 2020, the street name to which some had originally objected had become a source of community pride.

Ragged Ass Road has put Yellowknife on the map and made it the source of multiple pop culture references. For any skeptics who might remain resentful of the raunchy road name, there's an easy course of action to put things into perspective. The name which Ragged Ass replaced wasn't much better. The street used to be called Privy Road because there are so many outhouses on it.

As is often the case with great stories in the Northwest Territories, it all starts with a bunch of drunken gold prospectors. The group is led by a dude named Lou Rocher who owns six of the nine lots on Privy Road at the time. While drinking their blues away after a difficult prospecting season has yielded little income, Rocher jokes that since they are all "ragged ass broke," they might as well make that the name of the street. The gag catches on and Ragged Ass Road becomes the unofficial name. The men put up a sign that night.

For understandable reasons, the City of Yellowknife balks at putting up official street signs. But if you're a man who owns 67% of the property on any given road you sometimes feel empowered to take things into your own hands. Rocher makes sure his initiative will come to fruition.

He has road signs made and installs them himself. When they keep getting stolen he starts welding the signs to the posts. At that point Ragged Ass fever begins to catch fire in Yellowknife. Tourist shops all over town start selling t-shirts, stickers, and mock street signs bearing the name. Before long you can buy anything from a shot glass to a sugar bowl branded with the Ragged Ass logo.

Fueling the road's flame of fame were three specific events which achieved international pop culture references for Ragged Ass. In chronological order you had the song & album, the airline incident, and the book reference.

SONG & ALBUM ~ In 1995 former Red Rider lead singer, Tom Cochrane, named his third album *Ragged Ass Road* after the street. The title track of the album described a place "Where the shore fires burn out on a new frontier," and had the chorus "Oh did you find the midnight sun, Down on Ragged Ass Road?"

It added to the road's allure as a tourist attraction, but the city still demurred from making the name official. Cochrane went on to be inducted into the Canadian Music Hall of Fame.

WESTJET UPSET ~ In the spring of 2012, a British Columbia man flying out of Vancouver on WestJet with a Ragged Ass Road T-shirt was told by a flight attendant to either cover it up or turn it inside out for the duration of the flight since the airline was "family-friendly." He chose the former option, but when the incident made national news, WestJet apologized. And how's this for irony?

When it did so, WestJet posted to its Instagram account a photo of a Ragged Ass Road sign that had been on the office wall of its chief executive officer, Gregg Saretsky, for two years! Yellowknife city officials made it a point to meet with WestJet officials to come to a common understanding: the T-shirts are a tourist draw to be tolerated.

THE BOOK NOOK ~ August 2012 saw the release of a crime novel called *Bones Are Forever* which is partially set in Yellowknife. Author Kathy Reichs, a producer of the American television series *Bones*, had attended the NorthWords Literary Festival in Yellowknife in 2011 and liked the city so much she wrote it into her next novel.

In one scene her main character, Temperance Brennan, trails a suspect from downtown Yellowknife to Ragged Ass Road on a cold morning, giving her a chance to offer a detailed description in which she summarizes the prevailing architectural style of Ragged Ass as "northern hodgepodge." Here is a condensed version for Reichs' description of Ragged Ass Road:

"A sign on a rock said Ragged Ass Road. That's one you'd never see on the Queen City map... The neighborhood was residential, with browned-out grass hugging up to the road and utility wires hanging low overhead. I smelled fishy water and bracken mud, and sensed a lake nearby ... The newer homes looked like they'd been assembled from mail-order kits. Aluminum siding. Prefab windows. Faux-colonial shutters and doors... The older ones resembled cottages at a hippie summer camp. Unstained frame exteriors painted with murals or images taken from nature. Metal downspouts and smokestacks. Whirligigs, plastic animals, and ceramic gnomes in the yards or topping the fence ... Every house had at least one outbuilding, a rusted tank, and a mound of firewood."

Lou Rocher died in May 2013 and was remembered around Yellowknife most prominently for giving Ragged Ass Road its name. Despite that, his family noted, at that time the city still had not installed official street signs with the name. In 2015 official Ragged Ass Road signs were erected at both ends of the road. Sometimes you have to die to get your due.

Flight attendant with his balls of brass
Said, "Take off that shirt, it's so crass"
But times they would change
And rules rearrange
Now they all love the road Ragged Ass

SUPERIOR BOTTOM, WEST VIRGINIA

Located in southwest West Virginia, here's a town that's got you covered high and low. Within Superior Bottom runs Island Creek and keeping things safe on that Waterway is the beacon emanating from God's Lighthouse. Honest to God.

Chapter 17
OOH, THAT'S GROSS

Yes, there really is a town in West Virginia named **Booger Hole**. Confronting our fear of flatulence, we will visit both **Middelfart** and **Brokenwind**. Our sophomoric antics will include **Pee Pee** and **Poo Poo**. And you know what? If you don't like it, we don't give a **Shit**, or a **Shitterton** for that matter.

> *The Boogerhole murders chagrined*
> *The Shitterton sign stealers sinned*
> *We can't Poo Poo Pee Pee*
> *So then I just guess we*
> *Leave Middelfart for Brokenwind*

BOOGER HOLE, WEST VIRGINIA

It seems that the town name of Booger Hole morphed out of the term "boogieman." People used that nickname in the early 1900's to describe a mysterious figure responsible for a spate of murders and disappearances, shrouding the community under a cloak of mystery, myth and blood-letting murder. The apex was reached in 1917. WWI may have been ending but trouble in Booger Hole, not so much.

During that year a dozen or more people were brutally murdered or disappeared in the Booger Hole backwoods, some of them women and children. Townspeople who were weary of the fear and trepidation in their community formed the Clay County Mob and posted notice in the newspaper stating they intended to drive murder and mayhem out of their community.

The announcement read, in part, "We have pledged our lives to drive these people from our county or kill them… if before you leave, there is any stealing, killing or burning, we will get the bloodhounds and detectives and run you to the ends of the earth."

Today, the town's a major destination for ghost hunters. Paranormal experts rate Booger Hole as one of the 20 most haunted places in America. No arguments here.

When the murders subsided, both unexplained and unresolved, the Appalachian community's optimism was expressed in a little ditty which became a local folk classic.

Goin' up to Booger Hole, goin' in a run,
Goin' up to Booger Hole to have a little fun.
Goin' up to Booger Hole, goin' in a pace,
Rather go to Booger Hole than any other place.

Today, the community is filled with modern houses and well-kept farms, with little hint of its treacherous past. But if you ever find yourself thinking you'd "rather go to Booger Hole than any other place," you may want to rethink.

BROKENWIND, SCOTLAND

The Hamlet of Brokenwind is located in the council area of Aberdeenshire, Scotland. Maps from the 19th century show the name spelled as "Broken Wynd," with "wynd" being a Scottish word for a narrow path that snakes or winds between two larger roads.

In a 2012 poll of the "Britain's Worst Place Names" Brokenwind came in third. What two names were deemed to be even worse? Those would be Scratchy Bottom and Shitterton.

MIDDELFART, DENMARK

Despite the flatulent name, Middelfart is actually a small thriving city in central Denmark with a population surpassing 15,000. Its name dates back to 1231 A.D. and is derived from the term "Melfar," a Danish word which means "middle crossing."

Middelfart was a hub for whale hunters from the Middle Ages until the end of the 19th century. Even though whaling became officially uncool in the 20th century, Middelfarters reverted to their old habits during both of the world wars.

The city is located on the northwestern tip of the Danish island of Funen. So one of the attractions of a visit to Middelfart is that in addition to giggling at the name and getting your picture taken at the sign, you get to have fun in Funen.

PEE PEE, OHIO

Pee Pee is a township in southeast Ohio with a population of almost 8,000 people. What we know for sure is that the name is a result of a man carving his initials into a beech tree. What's not so certain is which man it was, with there being two suspects in the running.

- Suspect #1 ~ town founder Major Paul Paine
- Suspect #2 ~ 19th century settler Peter Patrick

The actual carving was of just the letters "P.P." but somehow over time, after the moniker had been adopted as the town's name, the spelling morphed into Pee Pee. The name has also been adopted for the local waterway Pee Pee Creek.

Some locals think it's funny, while others would rather relieve themselves of the burden. In interviews we read, some natives admitted that they told outsiders that they lived in Waverly a village within the township of Pee Pee. Even though in actuality they don't live in Waverly, they live in Pee Pee.

In assessing the natives' take on their town name, we thought this quote from Peytan Raegan-Barker was interesting. "I don't really like my town having that name," she said, "but for some reason Pee Pee Creek bothers me even more. Not that I'd spend a lot of time in the creek anyway, but that name drives me right out of the water."

POO POO, HAWAII

Obviously this Hawaiian island does not have the most attractive of names in terms of being a tourist draw. But that's okay. If, while on your next Hawaiian vacation, your party suddenly decides to peruse Poo Poo, you'd soon discover that you were the only ones there. Poo Poo is an uninhabited island about five miles off the coast of Maui.

But don't poo poo Poo Poo. While there are no human inhabitants, the island features an attractive array of indigenous animals.

SHITTERTON, ENGLAND

In May of 2012, the chants of, "We're #1," could be heard ringing out in the streets of this hamlet in southwest England. What was the cause of this celebration? The *Find My Past* genealogy website's survey of "Britain's Worst Place Names" had placed Shitterton on top of the heap.

We've seen examples of how sometimes towns in foreign countries just accidentally end up with names that have funky meanings in English but no unusual meaning in the native language. But this town is in England so that's not the case here and Shitterton means pretty much just what it sounds like.

The name has been around for over a millennium and the Old English definition was "town located on an open sewer." In 1086, at the direction of King William the Conqueror, the Domesday Book or "Great Survey" of Britain was recorded. This was essentially a documentation of all the towns in the country and their populations.

At that point in time the town was recorded as Sciteton with the English root word of the first syllable on the verge of evolving into its modern-day form. So Shitterton has maintained its meaning for a long time and in the ultraconservative Victorian era of the 19th century an attempt was made to change the name to Sitterton. Turns out that didn't sit well with the Shittertonians and the name reverted to its original form.

As we've seen to be the case with many of the uniquely named towns we've covered, the Shitterton sign was a frequent target of theft until 2010. That was the year the Parish Council took a proactive approach to dealing with the problem. They bought a 1.7 ton chunk of polished rock onto which they engraved the town's name.

Parish Council Chairman Ian Ventham aptly justified the council's significant investment in the new signage. Ventham explained, "We thought, 'Let's put in a ton and a half of stone and see them try and take that away in the back of a Ford Fiesta.'"

SHIT, IRAN

If you've always felt Iran was full of shit, please allow the map of world geography to provide your confirmation. In accessing the international atlas an index will confirm the following fact. There are only two places on the planet named "Shit" and they are both in Iran. Not a lot to differentiate the two except for a few hundred miles and some mosques.

The biggest difference might be that the one in the north has a population of about a thousand and the one in the west has a population of 300. This has led to one of the most common Iranian jokes amongst Uber drivers. Upon receiving calls with perhaps confusing destinations those Arab pranksters will respond by saying, "Did you get called to the Big Shit or the Little Shit?" Apparently the humor in this never grows old.

Chapter 18
BATMAN, THE DARK KNIGHT

We've always been huge bat fans ever since the campy 1960's Adam West TV series. So when we stumbled across the fact that there's a place in North Carolina called **Bat Cave**, we could not resist the urge to flesh out that concept for a complete chapter. The results were rousing.

We traveled to **Gotham** to confront the **Penguin** at **Joker Mine**. Appropriately, however, the most intriguing storyline emerged from **Batman** itself. There's a town in Turkey that bears that name and has taken on a somewhat bizarre relationship with the Caped Crusader. We'll tell you about how they've done all of the following.

- Sued Warner Bros. over the movies.
- Blamed Batman for an increased teen suicide rate.
- Attempted to gerrymander its boundary to the shape of the Bat-Signal.

BAT CAVE, NORTH CAROLINA

While it sounds like a cool place for Batman and Robin to hang out, Bat Cave, North Carolina is actually a quaint picturesque community located in the Appalachian Mountains of western North Carolina. It's a half-hour drive from Asheville which has always been considered North Carolina's hippest city.

The name is reality based. Bat Cave is the home of North America's largest known granite fissure cave. The cave itself is located inside Bluerock Mountain just north of Lake Lure. The main chamber inside the cave is a dark cathedral more than 300 feet long and 85 feet high. Hikers used to be able to enter the cave, but that's no longer the case.

Among the many species of bats inhabiting the cave is the endangered "Indiana bat" which is susceptible to a disease called "white nose syndrome." Zoologists determined that human traffic contributed to the spread of the disease, hence prohibiting hikers from the hangout.

If you're into ethnic diversity Bat Cave may not be your cup of tea. The population numbers 176, of whom 174 are white. While your first assumption might be that those remaining two would perhaps be one African-American couple that would be incorrect. There is one Asian dude and one Native American chick. No word on whether they're dating.

The downtown section of Bat Cave features a cider mill, antique shop, volunteer fire department, post office and there is a bimonthly community paper called "The Bat Biz."

GOTHAM, WISCONSIN

With the multiple incarnations of the Batman story having so ingrained "Gotham City" into our lexicon, it's perhaps surprising that there's only one place in the United States which features the word "Gotham" in its name. Gotham is a small town, population 191, located about dead center in the state of Wisconsin. Milwaukee and Lake Michigan are directly east, about 75 miles away.

The town was named after Captain Myron Gotham who died when his ship sank in Lake Michigan in 1902. If any seafaring captain ever deserved to be saved by our favorite superhero it was probably Gotham. Unfortunately, however, Bill Kane would not create the character Batman until 1939, three decades too late to get the job done.

JOKER MINE, ARIZONA

For better or worse, no jokes have been played here since 1930. The small settlement sprang up in the 1860's to mine granite in the Weaver Mountains near Meadview, Arizona which is in the northwest corner of the state not far from the Nevada border. Mining operations continued on and off until 1930. Of the first great actors to play the Joker, Cesar Romero, born in 1907, could have visited his mine as a young man but it was closed by the time Jack Nicholson was born in 1937.

ALFRED, NEW YORK

Our son Skyler always loved the character of Alfred the Butler in the Batman Universe, so we felt obligated to give a quick shout out to this college town located in upstate New York. Actually only two hours south of us, Alfred is the home of two colleges: Alfred University (4-year school) and Alfred State College (2-year school).

Here's a weird perspective on the Alfred population. There are more kids at the colleges than there are people actually living in the town. While the combined college enrollment is approximately 6,000 the most recent Alfred census placed the resident population at about 4,000.

And in terms of population quirks let's carry it to the next degree. Permanent residents seem to be fleeing Alfred in droves. While the official 2010 census placed the population at 5,237, the 2016 census came in at 4,060. We have no inside info as to the reason why, but we do come to one common conclusion. If you're looking to get hired as a butler, Alfred is probably not the place to go.

PENGUIN, TASMANIA

Heretofore, the most famous animal associated with this island has certainly been the Tasmanian Devil, a ferocious mammal buoyed to fame by the classic Warner Bros. whirling dervish cartoon character. Before we move on from one animal to the next, in our constant efforts to inform as well as entertain, please allow us to provide a capsule description of a true-to-life Tasmanian devil for those of you whose only visual is the spinning cartoon character.

Just to give you a quick ID on the actual Tasmanian devil, it is a carnivorous marsupial that was once also native to mainland Australia but is now found in the wild only on the island state of Tasmania. The size of a small dog, the Tasmanian devil is known for its stocky muscular build, extremely loud and disturbing screech, and ferocity when feeding.

Returning to the Town of Penguin, it is a delightful seaside town on the Tasmanian north coast with a finely honed sense of humor about its name. The joy of a visit to Penguin is to admire and be amused by the endless number of ways the town celebrates the word "penguin." It has a quiet, serene charm which is a common feature of the coastal towns on this island which is located off the southeast coast of Australia. Tasmania is officially a part of Australia, being one of its six states.

No prizes for guessing how Penguin got its name as of course they're all over the place. The noted botanist, Robert Campbell Gunn, observing the large numbers of fairy penguins (sometimes called little penguins) along the coast decided that the name was appropriate. He named the settlement in 1861.

Since the town's name is Penguin then just about everything, particularly along the sea shore, is a celebration of penguins. Consequently there is the Big Penguin, community rubbish bins encased by penguins, and even the Penguin branch of Meals on Wheels has a penguin on the side of the building.

The main attraction is the little penguins which can be seen arriving each evening between November and March. Those penguins are actually alive, as opposed to the 10-foot high "Big Penguin" statue which was erected in 1975 and towers over the beachfront park providing plentiful penguin pic possibilities.

Our ideal "Big Penguin" pictures, although neither ever occurred as far as we know, would have been the big statue side-by-side with Burgess Meredith or Danny DeVito.

BATMAN, TURKEY

Batman is a city of about 350,000 located in southeast Turkey, within the province of Batman. For the record there's also a Batman River. Until the 1950's it was a small town of about 3,000. Then oil was discovered and all hell broke loose in Batman. As Robin, the Boy Wonder, might have said, "Holy 10,000% population increase, Batman!"

Any change that drastic is bound to bring some conflict and life in Batman was never a bowl of cherries to begin with. Its location is not far from the point where the borders of Turkey, Iraq and Syria come to a "T" so ethnic tension between the Turks and Kurds has always been in the equation here. But when the Kurds discovered oil and Batman was flooded by Turks looking to cash in on the potential profits, things got Arab ugly. In one year alone Batman had 180 murders, too many for even the greatest of crime fighters to handle.

The average temperature in the summer is 90° here, so one villain Batman rarely has to fend off is Mr. Freeze. Just to show that the natives are aware that their city shares a name with an American superhero, in 2008 then-mayor Hüseyin Kalkan, sued Warner Bros. over their use of the name "Batman" in *The Dark Knight* trilogy. "There is only one Batman in the world," he declared. "The American producers used the name of our city without informing us."

Kalkan went as far as to blame a number of unsolved murders, as well as a high rate of suicide among young women, on the psychological impact that *The Dark Knight* films inflicted on his city's inhabitants.

"We expect a huge compensation from this," he declared, pledging to use the money to help women and street children. The mayor was laughed out of court and then out of office.

> *Batman, Turkey's a place where they lied*
> *Sued Warners but they were denied*
> *Stuck to their claim for*
> *Pinning the blame for*
> *Their wave of increased suicide*

PETITION DRIVE ~ But the fervor of bat-fever was far from finished. The Turks and the Kurds don't agree on much but the one cause they could coalesce upon was a joint initiative to gerrymander the map and have the province boundaries reconfigured into the shape of the Bat-Signal. In fairness to its neighbors, a petition was initiated that calls for Batman to acquire and concede equal amounts of land in order to achieve the reconfiguration.

We have signed the petition and urge you, our readers, to join the cause. You can sign the petition online. The whole web address is long but if you just enter "Batman Turkey petition" it will come up. As of now we have 27,000 signatures and if we can get to 35,000 the petition can be submitted to the governor of Batman for consideration.

BAT-SWAG ~ In 2007 Turkey started an institution of higher learning in the city which of course bears the name Batman University. We hear the sweatshirts are really cool!

CHAPTER 19
A ZOOTOPIAN EXPERIENCE

This chapter has our single favorite segment in the book, but we've got a few critters to cover before we get to our fave. We'll supply the details and let you decide if you'd rather eat **Rabbit Hash** or a diet of **Worms**. We'll ponder the question of whether a **Bird-in-Hand** is worth a **Monkey's Eyebrow**. But best of all, we're going to head up north to **Chicken**, Alaska. Nobody on the planet has embraced their quirky name to the point this place has. Their website is hilarious and perhaps most titillating of all, they have a panty cannon. We're sure you'll want to experience the delicious details of that one!

MONKEY'S EYEBROW, KENTUCKY

Monkey's Eyebrow is a rural community in western Kentucky, Ballard County to be precise. There's plenty of wildlife in these parts – deer, coyotes, wolves, muskrat and mink – but no monkeys. So how did the town get its quirky name? We found three different theories regarding the origin of the community's unique moniker. We'll share them with you and give you our selection for the one to go with. The Monkey's Uncle, so to speak.

Theory #1 - One theory on the origin of this unusual name is that when looking at Ballard County on a map, it resembles a monkey's head. Based upon the shape of the hypothetical head, the location of Monkey's Eyebrow within the county is about where the monkey's eyebrow would theoretically be.

Theory #2 - The second theory states that if you stand on the top of the hill overlooking the town and peer down at it, the town looks like it's in the shape of a monkey's eyebrow.

Theory #3 - Yet another theory of the town's naming is that sometime during the late 1800's, a community resident hated the local general store owners and subsequently shopped out of town. The man so despised the store owners he called the place "only fit for a bunch of monkeys," and compared the owners to primates who had eyebrows like monkeys.

So which theory do you buy into? Here's our take on it. There's an inherent flaw in Theories #2 & #3 which both involve something looking like a monkey's eyebrow. Monkeys don't have eyebrows, so we're going to throw our support to Theory #1.

RABBIT HASH, KENTUCKY

Located in the northernmost county in Kentucky, Rabbit Hash is a small town with a population of 315. While it may be small in size, it's large in storylines. In addition to its unusual name, Rabbit Hash has one of the country's most historic general stores and since 1998, the town has elected a dog to the office of mayor. The incumbent canine is a pit bull named Brynneth Pawltro. Rabbit Hash is rabidly humorous!

The beginning of the general store story predates the story of how the town got its name so we'll start with the store, hit the hash, then deal with the dogs. The hamlet's most notable building, the Rabbit Hash General Store, was built around 1831 and regarded as "the best known and best preserved country store in Kentucky."

The store was added to the National Register of Historic Places on February 2, 1989. On February 13, 2016, the famous General Store was decimated by a fire, and the subsequent mayoral elections were enhanced to act as a fundraising mechanism to restore the building.

Using a combination of original material and donor lumber from other period-correct structures around the area, the restoration was completed and the Rabbit Hash General Store reopened on April Fools' Day, 2017. The use of the vintage lumber enabled the store to maintain its historic designation. The refurbished general store, in addition to in-house food service, also allows menu items to go through the Scalded Hog Takeout.

NEW NAME ~ Let's move on to the town's name. According to popular legend, a flood in the 1840's drove hundreds of rabbits from the riverbank, and right into the stew pots of hungry settlers. It was rabbit hash all around. During that era the town was known as Carlton.

Because mail was being mixed up with the larger community of Carrollton, several miles down the Ohio River, the post office mandated that Carlton come up with a new name and since the rabbit hash story had become embedded in local lore, citizens decided to christen the town Rabbit Hash, Kentucky.

CANINE MAYORS ~ The first elected mayor in Rabbit Hash history was an adopted dog "of unknown parentage" named Goofy Borneman-Calhoun, who was inaugurated in 1998 for a four-year term. Goofy died in office in July 2001 at the age of 16.

The mayoralty remained unfilled until the next election, held in 2004, at which time Junior Cochran, a black Labrador, assumed office. Junior came under the scrutiny of the Northern Kentucky Health Department and was banned from entering the Rabbit Hash General Store due to complaints.

According to a TV news report of March 13, 2008, the dog's owner petitioned the court for an exemption for the "mayor." Perhaps due to the stress of the legal proceedings, it was shortly thereafter reported that Junior had died in office on May 30 at the age of 15.

After spending most of the summer without a mayor, a special election was held on August 31, 2008 to fill the vacancy left by Mayor Junior's death. This was won by Lucy Lou, a border collie who became the town's first female mayor.

Lucy Lou turned out to be a groundbreaking politician in more than one regard. She became the first celebrity from Rabbit Hash to make a network TV appearance, sharing a "Talking Points" walk with Willie Geist on *CBS Sunday Morning*. After that Lucy went on to prove that she was one dog whose bite was every bit as loud as her bark. Check out this list of accomplishments she rattled off.

- Accepted a $1,000 stimulus check from *Reader's Digest* for the "We Hear You America Tour Campaign."
- Served as grand marshal of the Covington Paw-Rade.
- Appeared in a segment of the syndicated TV show *The List*.

- Placed 3 years in a row in the Best Elected Official category in *Cincinnati CityBeat* magazine's "Best of Cincinnati" issue (winning 1st place in 2013).

Mayor Lucy Lou's prominence probably pinnacled on September 7, 2015, when her office announced that she was considering a run for the presidency of the United States. After careful consideration, Lucy determined that the office was beneath her and decided to retire from politics altogether. While she became the first Rabbit Hash mayor to step down from office while still living, she actually died at the youngest age, passing away in 2018 at the age of 12. One accolade Lucy Lou could take to the grave with her... she certainly lived up to the promise she campaigned upon when she declared herself, "The Bitch you can count on."

After Lucy Lou's departure, a special mayoral election was held on November 8, 2016 to put the next pooch in power. As previously mentioned, this election became part of a fundraising effort to reconstruct the Rabbit Hash General Store which had recently burned. A pit bull named Brynneth Pawltro, or "Brynn" as her friends call her, took first place having raised $3,367 and was, at this writing, the current mayor of Rabbit Hash.

The Rabbit Hash dog / pony show
Dogs get their ducks all in a row
The town loved Lucy Lou
Who passed the baton to
A mayor who's named Brynneth Pawltro

Following in the footsteps of Gwyneth Paltro, the actress for whom she was named, Brynn parlayed her mayoral victory into the beginning of a TV career. Shortly after her *indawguration* in 2017, Brynneth Pawltro made a guest appearance in the ABC sitcom *The Mayor*. Let's just hope she doesn't suffer from being typecast.

WORMS, GERMANY

This makes it into the book for a short quirky reason. Here's the background to set up the punch line. During the era of the Holy Roman Empire, "diets" were meetings held to consider important political and religious questions. A diet was held in Worms in 1521 at which Martin Luther was declared a heretic.

That religious assembly had manifestations extending above and beyond the mysteries of life which we will attempt to resolve in this manuscript. But that meeting in the 16th century in Worms took on a name that warrants a modern day giggle. The Diet of 1521 was commonly referred to as *the* Diet of Worms. Subscribe to any diet plan you choose; this is a protein-laden calorie-cutter for sure!

CHICKEN, ALASKA

In our ongoing quest to tell the stories behind the most uniquely named places on the planet, rarely did we laugh as hard as we did when we visited the website for Chicken, Alaska. It is an enigmatic place with more stories in one town than there are eggs in a hen house. There are so many storylines, it's almost hard to know where to start.

Here are some of the fun facts you have to look forward to before departing for Chicken, Alaska. Did you know that the Gold Rush is still on in some parts of America? Did you know it is possible for a town with an official population of 7 to host one of the most hilarious websites around? Do you know what a Ptarmigan bird looks like? Well, the answers to all these questions and more can be found in Chicken, Alaska. Stay tuned.

EARLIEST ARRIVALS - The first people to arrive in town did so in the 1890's looking for gold. When enough people showed up to constitute a community, the decision was made to organize and come up with a name. In 1902, when Chicken was to become incorporated, it was only the second town in Alaska to do so, Juneau having incorporated in 1900. In that year the local post office was established requiring a community name and here's how that game played out here.

The name "Ptarmigan" was suggested because the area was home to many ptarmigans, which are a medium-sized gamebird in the grouse family, and the official state bird of Alaska. At that point in time there were three different spellings in use for the bird and some indecision about which one was actually correct.

Since ptarmigans look kind of like wild chickens, it was decided to incorporate using the word "Chicken" as the town's title, serving as a "placeholder," so to speak, until agreement could be reached upon which spelling of Ptarmigan would become the permanent town name.

Well, 120 years later they're still stickin' with Chicken. And that's a choice which is certainly validated by this very article you are reading. Ptarmigan, Alaska never would have made our survey of the quirkiest place names on the planet. Chicken, Alaska on the other hand is a choice we can cheer for.

CHICKEN FACTS ~ So anyway, let's return to the fun facts with which we challenged you above. Chicken, Alaska started out as a gold mining town and it remains true to those roots to this very day. That being said, the gold mining takes place on a seasonal basis which is part of what adds to the quirky charm of Chicken. The town is located way up there, in central eastern Alaska, and as the Chickenites say, it's cold in them thar hills. The average high in January is -14 and the average low is -31. The bone-chilling record low stands at -72.

With those frosty figures in mind, we think the summer stats will surprise you. Check out these average high temperatures... June~69, July~70, August~64. So clearly there's a chunk of the year when you could be out there in your short sleeves panning for gold. And there's still gold out there for the pickin' in Chicken.

So next we should probably provide a breakdown on how this seasonal thing works when you're within shouting distance of the Arctic Circle. Chicken is accessible by air via Chicken Airport, and by road via Alaska Route 5, the Taylor Highway, which is maintained from spring to early fall.

This highway is made of packed gravel regularly traveled by cars, trucks, and motor homes. Paving the road is in the discussion process with two primary offers under consideration. Pavement will happen when either,

#1) Pigs fly
#2) Hell freezes over.

We'll keep you posted.

So while there's never a plethora of people in Chicken, there's a drastic difference between winter and summer. In looking at the official census counts, the permanent population peaked at 41 in the 1940 census and by 2010 that permanent number was down to 7. The summer population was in the hundreds in the mid-20th century and still exceeds 100 in the modern era.

Add to that, the tourists and the summers in Chicken are still substantial enough to sustain their version of an Alaskan strip mall which includes a post office, bar, gift shop, café, and liquor store.

HOT TIPS - Here are our insider tips if you go to visit Downtown Chicken. If you hit the café, try some of Sue's famous cinnamon rolls which are incredible. Say hi to Sue, she's always there and she'll snicker if you call her by name. Then swing by the post office (delivering the mail since 1906) and say hi to Robin. She doesn't wear a name tag so if you call her Robin she'll know that you've been Chicken-savvy enough to visit the Chicken website to get the local lowdown.

Now that we've mentioned it, let's hit the Chicken website. Right off the bat, you'll be able to print out your online coupon which will reward you with a free gift immediately upon your entry into the gift shop. No spoiler alert here - we're not going to identify the free gift but know this, we have ours hanging in the front room and not a soul passes without commenting upon it.

But once you've printed out your Chicken coupon and headed for eastern Alaska to cash it in, there are a few things you'll need to block out of your mind. One of those would be the computer you just used, because the next thing we will share with you is the rundown of amenities unavailable in Chicken.

If after enjoying coffee and Sue's cinnamon roll at the bakery, you're thinking you're going to hit the bathroom before logging on to your computer to catch up with emails and then phoning a few friends to share the details of your awesome Alaskan experience, we've got some good news and bad news.

The good news is you'll have lots of free time on your hands because the bad news is none of those aforementioned communications options are available. And in terms of relieving yourself of Sue's coffee, that will not be happening at the comfortable inside restroom. The outside outhouse is just around the corner to your right. The list of amenities unavailable in Chicken includes phone service, internet, and running water; electricity is available only via generator.

No plumbing, don't be panic-stricken
But your pace to the outhouse might quicken
You're pissed off and swearing
But at least you're bearing
Gifts saying, "I got laid in Chicken!"

WEBSITE WINNERS ~ While exploring the Chicken Website, they have the almost-always included "FAQ" button. Not surprisingly, the Chicken website also includes a link for "NFAQ", translation – Not Frequently Asked Questions. These were all one-off questions sent to the Chicken site and the witty responses offered by web master Doug Devore. Of the dozens of "NFAQ" "Q&A"s here are our three favorites:

Q. I am worried that if we move to Chicken, my children will have to marry each other. What are your laws about inbreeding? *Jennifer, Virginia Beach, VA*
A. Jennifer, have you considered how convenient it would be to look for dates right at your family reunion?

Q. Do you eat a lot of chicken in Chicken? *Laura, St. Peter, MN*
A. With that assumption, I hate to think of what you do in St. Peter.

Q. Does everybody in Chicken wear that same red flannel shirt? *Jerry, Silicon Valley, CA*
A. Not at the same time.

These are all Honest-to-God transcriptions from the Chicken, Alaska message board.

We mentioned earlier in the piece how much fun the Chicken website is, so we led with that sample of three Q&A's to exemplify our point. Webmaster Doug Devore admits in his online Chicken bio that he is guilty of having a fowl sense of humor.

Another highlight of the website is that there is a continuously moving graphic where the heads of all the employees cycle through and appear above a red flannel shirt which remains stationary. This graphic would explain the basis for question #2 on the previous page.

There's also a nice variety of Chicken merchandise available including t-shirts, baseball caps, and beer koozies. Their #1 seller is what they refer to as their "famous and classy" t-shirt which shows a chicken breaking out of an egg with the caption "I got laid in Chicken." We're sure that's a goal shared by many but realized by few.

There is also information on cabin rentals and even an option to buy the entire downtown compound. The four commercial entities comprising beautiful downtown Chicken are the emporium, liquor store, saloon and café.

The website includes some titillating tidbits on what is included in the offer and what is not. For example, in the saloon the deal is "underwear stapled to the ceiling included ~ panty cannon is negotiable." For us, we're thinking the inclusion of the panty cannon would be pretty much a make-or-break component of the deal.

What does it cost to buy your own town in Alaska? For a mere $750,000 you can set yourself up in a business where you can make enough money in five months to afford to go on vacation for the remaining seven months of the year. Further sweetening the pot, if you buy the town you get 15% off the purchase of a t-shirt! You'd be pickin' a Chicken lickin' good deal!

We had so much fun perusing the Chicken website that we decided to call them and make friends. Turns out people in Chicken are as friendly in real life as they are on the internet. We spoke with Sue Wiren who is currently the owner of beautiful downtown Chicken. It was still winter and not yet Chicken Season when we spoke and Sue was at her ranch in Nevada.

She often spends her winters cruising the Caribbean but it was the 2020 winter of the pandemic when we first talked to her so there wasn't much cruising taking place. Here are some highlights from our question and answer session with Sue and don't worry, we did ask her the question we know has been lurking in the back of your mind since earlier in this segment, namely, "What's up with that panty cannon?!"

Q: When people come in the summer, where do they mostly stay? We saw cabin rentals available on your website, but we were wondering if people also drove in campers or pitched tents or what other options were available. How do people mine for gold in 2020? Is it still panning for gold like in the old movies?
A: Some people come for the whole summer as they want to strike it rich and mine gold. Most are suction dredgers who "vacuum" the bottom of streams and rivers for gold flakes and nuggets. Others work with bigger equipment that sits on the bank of the creek. Some people come in RV's, bicycles, pick-ups and cars. There are cabins and tent sites available in Town. We offer free camping and have a very nice cabin with an incredible view for rent.

Q: Does the plane fly in during the winter? How do the people who stay get food?
A: We get mail 2 times a week, summer and winter, by small plane. They fly as long as it is warmer than 40 below. Imagine a sleeping bag wrapped around the engine with a little heater inside the engine compartment. In the old days they would've drained the oil then put it back into the engine to start—when it was warm, of course. Wing covers protect the wings from ice and snow build up, which are removed before flight.

Q: And how profitable is it to mine for gold nowadays? Do some people make big bucks or is the "Chicken experience" more about the novelty of the outdoorsy, wilderness experience?
A: I never believe what gold miners tell me about what they are finding and I have no idea of the profitability. The ones who say nothing are the ones who come year after year and drive new trucks. Enough said. It is a small town. Do you routinely ask people, "How much do you make a

year?" Not done. It's not polite to ask. Some people do well and some people just pay for their gas but enjoy being on the river, living the dream, away from the hustle and bustle. It's nice there and it is a great place to spend the summer.

Q: How does the panty cannon work? (Obviously the most critical question of the bunch.) What is the backstory on the underwear on the ceiling?
A: The panty cannon is fired by black powder, and wadding partly comprised of panties. We also use a fuse so you can run like hell, once the fuse is lit. It is blown off in the parking lot and is not done on demand. It is the bartender's prerogative and is done for the pure fun and joy. The underwear on the ceiling and walls is what's left from the blast as a memorial to the party and its wearer.

More animal stories we've planned
Our Chicken piece turned out just grand
Mousie sounds fun
Big Beaver could run
A town that is called Bird-in-Hand

MOUSIE, KENTUCKY

With a population of about 1,600, Mousie is located in eastern Kentucky. Apparently parents in eastern Kentucky in the early 20th century had a strategy to assure that their daughters would not grow up to be mousy.

What was it? You named them Mousie. In 1916 in this Kentucky town when the first postmaster was charged with the task of coming up with a name for his town, he decided to keep it in-house. He named the town Mousie after his daughter Mousie Martin.

BIRD-IN-HAND, PENNSYLVANIA

Here's yet another Amish town in Pennsylvania with a curious name. With a population of about 400, Bird-in-Hand is located in the southeastern part of the state. Rather than send you on a wild goose chase, we're going to come right out and share the story of how the town got its name quoting directly from Bird-in-Hand's 250th anniversary handbook. The story dates back to 1734.

"The pike was being laid out in order to connect Lancaster with a direct route to Philadelphia. A discussion took place between two road surveyors as to whether they should stop at their present location or go on to Lancaster to spend the night.

One of them said, 'A bird in the hand is worth two in the bush.' The other surveyor followed this bit of advice and both remained at what became known as the Bird-in-Hand Inn."

It adds: "*It is known that the sign in front of the inn once portrayed a man with a bird in his hand and a bush nearby in which two birds were perched."* Here's a quick background on that idiom. Dating back to the ancient Greeks and first appearing in English around 1400, our choice explanation for what this idiom actually means is "having something, even if it is a lesser quantity, is better than taking the chance of losing it in order to attain something else that seems more desirable."

Chapter 20
JUSTIFYING THE JIM THORPE THEFT

WHAT'S IN A NAME? ~ Of all the locations we have ever visited, here is our most uniquely bizarre story regarding the naming of a place. Please join us in a somewhat creepy convoy to the Keystone State. Located deep in the heart of Pennsylvania is the picturesque town of Jim Thorpe. As one might suspect the town is named after the famous athlete, but the circumstances of how the town came to bear Jim Thorpe's name bizarrely border on the morbidly macabre.

Prior to Thorpe's death in 1953, the town was called Mauch Chunk. We kid you not. We challenge you to come up with two words and ten letters with a less appealing sound. The beauty and curse of that name is how it manages to get so ugly so quick. For example, if you wave the limit on letters you could come up with a two-word alternative name that might seem to mean about the same thing. How about Projectile Vomiting, PA? Not a lot of marketing potential in that one.

Any way you want to cut the Mauch Chunk cheese, this town is cursed with one of the ugliest sounding names ever. So what do the Mauch Chunkians do with their pukey Pennsylvania persona? Obviously it was going to take some initiative and ingenuity to dig out of this valley. They already have a truly picturesque town nestled amidst the peaks of the Pocono Mountains, and they come to the conclusion that their trending tourist trade could be terrifically touted if the town's name could be changed to have the travel brochures **not** sound like potential visitors need to bring their own vomit bags.

TIME FOR A CHANGE ~ But in order to set itself apart from the many other sleepy villages that dot the Poconos, Mauch Chunk knows it needs a name-changing/game-changing gimmick. What follows is a unique example of how quirkily the universe somehow aligns. We're halfway through the 20th century, the country is getting back on track after World War II, Mauch Chunk is looking for a new name, and legendary athlete Jim Thorpe dies.

How in the world do these dots connect? Well, the details of the negotiations are a bit murky but the long-story-short of it is that Jim Thorpe's widow, who was **not** the mother of any of his 8 children, agrees to sell her husband's corpse to Mauch Chunk for an undisclosed amount of money. The idea is that the town would entomb the body, erect the ultimate shrine for the sports legend, and rename the town "Jim Thorpe"; all of this despite the fact that Thorpe had never even personally been there.

Despite the objection of everyone else in Thorpe's family, as well as the obvious moral and ethical issues, Thorpe's wife did have the legal right to conduct this transaction. Thorpe's family has tried unsuccessfully from 1953 to this very day to have his remains returned to his native Oklahoma where they could be more appropriately buried. But the residents of the old Mauch Chunk obviously felt that the one-time expense of everybody having to ante up and buy new address labels was well worth it. They are keeping the body and keeping the name.

GREATEST OF ALL TIME ~ Jim Thorpe is considered by some to be the greatest athlete of all time. He played Major League Baseball and was also an early star in the NFL. Track and field may have been his best sport but he was great at everything from ballroom dancing to riding horses.

The opinion of who is the greatest athlete ever could be debated indefinitely with valid cases to be made for multiple candidates. But we are going to go out on a limb and, greatest athlete debate notwithstanding, we are going to say that without a doubt the greatest single year ever experienced by an all-around athlete was what Jim Thorpe accomplished in 1912.

In the spring of that year he won the college ballroom dancing championship (who would have thought that they even had such a thing at that time?). In the summer he sailed to Stockholm and won the Olympic gold medals in both the pentathlon and decathlon. He then returned home in the fall to lead his team to the national collegiate football championship. How's that for having a good year?!

Of course the real glory was still awaiting him when 50 years later a small town in Pennsylvania would come to bear his name.

Pennsylvania, sometimes the mind warps
Things can change at the drop of a corpse
Mauch Chunk go away
We've a new name to say
That's because the dead corpse was Jim Thorpe's

CHAPTER 21
HOME FOR THE HOLIDAYS

For some people on the planet the song "There's No Place Like Home For the Holidays" takes on a whole different meaning. Their towns' Christmas-themed monikers make them merry 365 days a year.

In an escalating layer of holiday hilarity we'll share with you the stories of one **Christmas**, two **North Poles**, and three **Santa Claus**es, all in the United States. After that we'll fly across the pond to England for dessert. What's on the menu there? How about a nice big slice of **Christmas Pie** on **Christmas Island**?

On the rooftop sometimes Santa pauses
Naming places with holiday causes
Our one "Christmas" extols
There are two "North Poles"
And then alas three "Santa Clauses"

SANTA CLAUS, INDIANA

Of the three towns in the United States with this name, Santa Claus, Indiana rises to the top of the chimney as the only one to have an official post office bearing the jolly name. The Santa Claus in Georgia is part of a larger post office and the one in Arizona is now a ghost town. Furthermore, the USPS has gone on record as saying that no other community will ever be allowed to use the name of Santa Claus.

It all started in 1854 when a group of settlers set up shop in southwest Indiana calling their town Santa Fe. A couple of years later it was time to procure a post office and an application was submitted to the state. There was good news and bad news. The good news was since they'd only been using their name for two years they hadn't become too attached, but the bad news came back that it was "No way, Santa Fe." Indiana already had a town by that name.

So, it was back to the drawing board and there are multiple accounts about what happened next. Combining components of various versions here's the most fancifully fun.

The townspeople held several meetings over the next few months to select a new name, but could not agree on one. The next town meeting was scheduled for December 24, prior to the Christmas Eve church service. During the discussion, the church doors were blown open by a gust of wind and the ringing of sleigh bells could be heard in the distance.

Several people, including children at the meeting, got excited and someone shouted "Santa Claus!" Before the jolly fat man arrived at midnight he'd have a town named after him. It was Santa Claus, Indiana, indeed!

In a tradition that dates back to the early 1900's, every year the town answers thousands of letters to Santa which come from all over the world. A legion of volunteer elves is recruited to complete the mission which certainly serves to bolster business for the local post office. For these efforts, in 1929 Santa Claus was saluted by *Ripley's Believe It or Not.*

On December 25, 1935, a 22-foot tall statue of Santa Claus was dedicated to the town and erected on its highest hill. The 40-ton concrete statue was restored in 2011, and in 2012, an historic local church and the town's original post office were moved to the site next to the large Santa Claus statue.

Proclaiming itself the place "where it's Christmas all year round," Santa Claus is the home to numerous themed attractions including: Santa's Candy Castle, the Santa Claus Museum, Holiday World & Splashin' Safari, Frosty's Fun Center, Christmas Lake Golf Course, and Santa's Stables. It is also home to Santa's Lodge and the Lake Rudolph Campground & RV Resort.

Here's one quirky Santa Claus sports stat. For a town that didn't have a thousand people until the 21st century, it was the home of an NBA head coach and two NFL quarterbacks. Native Del Harris coached the NBA Houston Rockets, Milwaukee Bucks and Los Angeles Lakers. Santa Claus's NFL quarterbacks were Jay Cutler who played for the Denver Broncos, Chicago Bears, and Miami Dolphins and Bob Griese who led the Miami Dolphins to the only perfect season in NFL history.

The town has seen considerable growth in recent decades, due largely to the expansion of the gated community of Christmas Lake Village. The census, which was around 900 in 1990 had risen to 2,500 by 2020. Seems that not only is Santa Claus coming to town, the town is coming to Santa Claus.

NORTH POLE, NEW YORK

North Pole is a small hamlet located in Adirondack Park near Whiteface Mountain, 12 miles from Lake Placid and approximately 30 miles from Plattsburgh. North Pole, as you might suspect, is one of the best places in the Northeast for snow. Your chances of a white Christmas in North Pole are 96%. In the official census North Pole is considered part of Lake Placid, so there are no specific population figures but only four houses remain around the intersection which constitutes the crossroads of the community.

There are only two commercial establishments remaining in the hamlet. North Pole has a small community post office at 201 Main St, which is open only on a seasonal basis. North Pole, New York's main attraction is Santa's Workshop on Whiteface Mountain Memorial Highway, Route 431.

Santa's Workshop is a timeless fantasy village which opened in 1949 as one of the country's first theme parks. Today it is the oldest operating theme park in the United States. Santa's Workshop has remained true to its original design to allow children of all ages to create the fantasy of Santa's Workshop. You will not find large amusement rides or high tech gadgets, but you will be able to visit with Santa, pet and feed his live Reindeer Team, play with all of Santa's Helpers and even touch the frozen North Pole. There are reindeer games for the whole family.

While North Pole, New York should be noted for its historical theme park status, it must be acknowledged that the North Pole, Alaska storyline is the more substantial. Keep reading our Christmas chapter to explore that option.

SANTA CLAUS, GEORGIA

Located halfway between Macon and Savannah, Santa Claus is a small town of 165 people in southeast Georgia. All of the streets have

Christmas-theme names like Candy Cane Road, Rudolph Way, and Sleigh Street.

The name Santa Claus was a 1930's brainstorm of a local entrepreneur, C.G. Greene, whose goal it was to lure travelers off the highway to visit his pecan stand and adjacent motel. At the time, the town sat right on U.S. 1, and there was a hope the small community could turn itself into some kind of a tourist attraction. Then the interstates came. Interstate 75 to the west and 95 to the east were too far away for Santa Claus to become a viable tourist attraction.

But that didn't put a dent in the residents' holiday spirit. When they built their new Town Hall it went up at 25 December Drive. In 2014, residents built a 40-seat chapel surrounded by a prayer garden. At Christmastime, when it is decorated with red bows and holly, the quaint little chapel makes the perfect photo op. The Santa Claus Chapel is located at 15 Holly Street.

While Santa Claus, Indiana, may be more famous, Santa Claus, Georgia, has plenty of holiday spirit. The town adopted the motto, "Santa Claus... The City That Loves Children" and put it on a sign that welcomes people to town, while simultaneously providing yet another photo op. If you live in Georgia and are looking for a location for that perfect picture for your family Christmas card, Santa Claus should be in your future.

CHRISTMAS, FLORIDA

If you're looking for Christmas all year round, head for this town of 1,100 in central Florida, about 25 miles east of Orlando. No matter what day of the year it is, you could find yourself rockin' around the Christmas tree at the 4-corners. As the sign there proclaims… "The permanent Christmas tree at Christmas, Florida is the symbol of love and good will; the Christmas Spirit every day in the year." The tree is accompanied by a painted concrete Santa Claus statue, a red wood sleigh and reindeer, and a nativity scene.

After you've celebrated the holiday, there's one more must-see attraction in Christmas, Florida. The town is home to the world's largest alligator! This beast, named Swampy, is a 200-foot long building, built in the shape of an alligator, which houses a zoo called Jungle Adventures - A Real Florida Animal Park. If you find yourself hankering to hold a real baby alligator, then this is the place for you.

NORTH POLE, ALASKA

Officially a "city" of just under 2,000 people, North Pole is located 13 miles southeast of Fairbanks and 1,700 miles south of the real deal. The real North Pole that is. It does qualify as somewhat of a modern-day success story. In 1944 the entire area was nothing but a marsh, covered with scrub trees and brush with nary a manmade structure in sight. Here's the story of how this Christmas village emerged from nothingness.

In 1891 Congress enacted legislation for town sites to be laid out in Alaska under regulations specified by the Secretary of the Interior. At that point the land that would become North Pole was officially for sale. While the territory featured a wildlife menagerie including moose, deer, foxes, wolves, beavers and snowshoe rabbits; potential buyers were not forming a line. As a matter of fact, it would take over half a century to cement the sale.

On April 7, 1944, Bob & Bernice Davis arrived in Fairbanks and drove into the countryside looking for a spot where they could live off the land. They found an available parcel at what would one day become North Pole. Little did they dream that their undistinguished 160 acres of scrub trees and brush would ever be more than just a homestead, much less that it would one day be called a city, let alone a city called North Pole.

The Davises gradually began to sell off pieces of their property to others interested in setting up stakes in this rural area outside of Fairbanks. In 1949, the National Board of Geographic Names assigned the name "Davis" to the parcel, attributing it to the couple that had purchased the land. In 1951, when it was determined that electricity would be installed, the value of the property increased significantly.

In February of 1952 the Dahl and Gaske Development Company bought all of the remaining land available. The company thought that if the growing settlement was named North Pole it might be able to attract business. They reasoned that some toy manufacturer might be induced to locate a factory there so their products could be advertised as being literally "made at North Pole." Another thought was that someone might start a Santa Land that could become a northern version of Disneyland which was under construction in California at the time.

The company approached Bob Davis to ask him about changing the name of the parcel from "Davis" to "North Pole." Davis thought that the idea was far-fetched but acceded to their request and the legal process was initiated to change the name. On January 15, 1953 a decree was issued making North Pole the official name of the community.

Nothing materialized in terms of the toy factory or theme park, but North Pole continued to grow and there was continued interest in developing North Pole as a theme city, "where the spirit of Christmas lives year round."

Today, many streets within North Pole bear holiday names such as Kris Kringle St. and Mistletoe St., and there's also Santa Claus Lane, Snowman Lane, Holiday Road and Saint Nicholas Drive. Street lights are decorated in candy cane motifs and many buildings are painted with Christmas colors and designs.

Each year the North Pole community starts the holiday season with a Winter Festival including fireworks, a candle lighting ceremony, an ice-carving festival and a community tree lighting in December. The Santa Claus House, the "official" home of Santa Claus, greets all visitors who pass through the city on the Richardson Highway.

The Santa Claus House is North Pole's biggest attraction. It's a modern-day incarnation of a trading post (gift shop) established in the town's early days. Made of fiberglass, and standing outside the establishment, is the world's largest statue of Santa Claus. Live reindeer and an opportunity for a photograph with Santa Claus are available year round.

The city's fire trucks and ambulances are all red, while the police cars are green and white. The city also has an all-female flat-track Roller Derby league, the North Pole Babes in Toyland whose athletes have Christmas and North Pole-inspired skater names.

Prior to Christmas each year, the USPS post office in North Pole receives hundreds of thousands of letters to Santa Claus, and thousands more from people wanting the town's postmark on their Christmas greeting cards to their families. It advertises the ZIP code 99705 as the ZIP code of Santa. A community program also responds to letters addressed to 1 Santa Claus Lane. There truly is no place like the North Pole.

SANTA CLAUS, ARIZONA

You'll find no shortage of ghost towns along Route 66, but one of the strangest by far has to be the abandoned town of Santa Claus, Arizona. The Mojave Desert, with its blisteringly hot summer sun, Joshua trees and bizarre rock formations, would not generally be the place one would choose to honor a man whose traditional home is the North Pole. Yet standing in the desert are the ghostly remnants of Santa Claus, Arizona.

Once a bustling, year-round holiday-themed stop for road-tripping motorists, its glory days are long past. Sadly, and ironically, the rattlesnakes now outnumber the reindeer in the ramshackle ruins remaining here. The rise and fall of Santa Claus, Arizona is a tale that truly tugs at your heartstrings. This one got to us a little bit and we look forward to sharing the story with you. Let's take a chronological look.

BEGINNING THROUGH 1950 ~ Santa Claus was founded in 1937 by an eccentric realtor named Nina Talbot who moved from California to Arizona. She billed herself as the biggest real estate agent in California, which might have come off as just egotistical were it not for the fact her weight of 300 pounds certainly added an air of duplicity to the claim.

She hoped to create a resort town in the Arizona desert, curiously provide her destination with a Christmas theme, and use the whole shebang to launch a real estate scheme which included subdividing her 80-acre parcel into individual lots. Her plan for the holiday-themed attractions to bring people to the town was an idea that surprisingly enough worked, sort of, at least for a while. Here's the scoop.

The land purchased by Talbot was located 14 miles northwest of Kingman, Arizona. On the property Talbot built a series of buildings employing her Christmas theme which included Santa's Workshop at the North Pole, and Cinderella's Doll House which had the look of a Swiss chalet. The post office was bustling, there was a live Santa Claus on call 365 days a year, and overnight accommodations were available in the Kit Carson Guest House which was part of the Santa Claus Inn. There were also Christmas related buildings and attractions.

The inn did a lucrative restaurant business with a favorite being the bargained priced "Big Farm Breakfast" which was available for just 75¢. Holiday-themed menu items included "Chicken à la North Pole" and "Rum Pie à la Kris Kringle." Another attraction was that the inn was air-conditioned, by no means a given during that era.

Nina Talbott's girth gave her a bit of a Mrs. Santa Claus vibe and that, combined with her acknowledged flair for public relations, put Santa Claus on the map, literally as well as figuratively. She had taken 80 acres of parched desert and turned it into a full-fledged tourist attraction. For Americans looking to get their kicks on Route 66, Santa Claus, Arizona was a spot not to be missed.

Talbott operated the town for a dozen years and while establishing a hit show in terms of tourism, one aspect of her original plan never materialized. The whole real estate component whereby individual plots of her 80 acres were going to be sold and developed did not happen. That was her wish, but of course we know that if wishes were dollars paupers would be kings. In 1949 she sold the whole town as a package which featured a hotel, restaurant and tourist attraction to Deb Douglas.

1950's ~ During the 1950's, Santa Claus, Arizona continued to capture the fancy of the American public. It did receive some high profile support in this regard. It was acknowledged by highly regarded authors, famous movie stars and celebrity chefs.

The decade began with famed science fiction writer Robert A. Heinlein using Santa Claus as the setting for a short story he wrote called *Cliff and the Calories*. In the story, Heinlein describes a sumptuous gourmet feast served by Mrs. Claus, who in reality would have been Mrs. Douglas, who ran The Santa Claus Inn restaurant in the 1950's. For what it's worth, this decade saw the Santa Claus Inn being renamed as the Christmas Tree Inn.

Well known restaurant critic Duncan Hines, who would later become famous for the brand of food products that bears his name, described the establishment as being the best in the region. About the restaurant Hines wrote that the Christmas Tree Inn was one of, "the best eating places along Arizona State Route 66."

In the perfect Christmas cliché, this type of celebrity attention had a snowball effect of which we will provide you one superlative example. At the top of the Hollywood diva list of the era was Jane Russell who, along with Marilyn Monroe, had co-starred in the megahit movie *Gentlemen Prefer Blondes* in 1953. On August 5, 1954, Russell had a party of ten friends driven from L.A. to Santa Claus, Arizona for a dinner party at the Christmas Tree Inn.

1960's ~ Business remained steady through the 1960's. In trying to recreate the era when Route 66 was the legendary east/west thoroughfare in the U.S. it would be kitschy stops like Santa Claus that would best epitomize the stereotypes and social nuances of that era.

For those of you too young to remember its glory days, *Route 66* was so high profile at the time it warranted its own TV series which ran on CBS for four years, from 1960-64. The show, which had a killer theme song, followed the adventures of two young men traversing the United States in a Chevrolet Corvette convertible, and the events and consequences surrounding their journeys.

1970's ~ The popularity of Santa Claus declined in the 1970's and the complex began to fall into disrepair. By the mid-1970's the main attractions had all closed down and the town was removed from the maps of Arizona. The early goal of attracting residents, other than the people who worked there, had never materialized and never would.

1980's ~ In July of 1983, owner Tony Wilcox offered to sell the remaining four acres which comprised Santa Claus for $95,000 but had no takers. He did receive one offer of $50,000, but turned it down, feeling certain that the remnants of the town were worth more.

By 1988 his asking price was down to $52,500. What remained at that point were three dilapidated A-frame buildings which had been painted to look like peppermint candies. These three buildings housed a restaurant, gift shop, and some children's attractions. Writer Mark

Winegardner visited Santa Claus in 1988 and wrote poignantly about the experience in his book *Elvis Presley Boulevard: From Sea to Shining Sea, Almost.* Here's what Winegardner saw.

> "Styrofoam silver bells, strands of burned-out Christmas lights and faded plastic likenesses of Old Saint Nick garnished this little village. A lopsided, artificial twenty-foot tree whistled in the wind beside a broken Coke machine and an empty ice freezer. Two of the three buildings were padlocked; through their windows, encrusted with layers of sand and decade-old aerosol snow, I saw dusty, overturned fiberglass statuettes of elves and reindeer. Alongside the SANTA CLAUS, ARIZONA / ESTABLISHED 1937 sign was another: FOR SALE BY OWNER / $52,500 / INQUIRE AT GIFT SHOP. An arrow pointed that way."
>
> "The gift shop stocked no seasonal items. Its shelves were littered with flea-market knickknacks at antique-shop prices. Battered paperbacks cost a buck. What little money the place generated must have come from the short-order grill and the soft-drinks cooler. On a stool behind the countertop cash register, a haggard, fiftyish man looked up from his circle-the-word puzzle and asked if we needed anything."

1990's ~ In the early 1990's, during the last days of the restaurant, a sampling of menu offerings included the Dasher and Dancer omelet and Santa Claus burgers. Oil portraits on black velvet of John Wayne could be purchased from the gift shop, and there were some nominal child amusements still in operation. As of 1995 everything was closed.

By the end of that decade Santa Claus featured just a few vandalized buildings, a wishing well, and the "Old 1225," a derailed, pink children's train covered with graffiti. The date of 12/25 no longer held significance to the "Old 1225."

2000's ~ The pink train lasted into the 2000's, although further marred and tagged with graffiti. By 2002, the train was gone and any remaining structures had been vandalized and well-worn by the weather. In 2003, the population of Santa Claus was 10, divided among five houses, one of which had a live buffalo.

By 2004, the town was identified as "an abandoned, road-pull-off, with a handful of old buildings – all closed, with 'This is it! Santa's Land'

and 'Santa's Desert Retreat' being the only two signs left from the early days of the town."

2010's ~ As of 2015, someone described Santa Claus, Arizona by saying, "Little remains of Santa Land. It's just two boarded-up, graffitied buildings. The train is gone, and there is little that remains of the special town. Someone even stole the face of Santa off the front sign."

As of 2017 a visitor described it as now being surrounded by a barbed wire fence having a huge gate that easily opened. The visitor, noticing a squatter residing in a remaining structure, jokingly chooses to opt out of the meet and greet. The formerly festive red and white candy peppermint paint jobs are just faintly visible behind the layers of graffiti. It's such a heartbreaking ending for an establishment that brought so much Christmas joy to so many people over the years. Guess that's what happens when you stop believing in Santa Claus.

The restaurant had cakes, shakes and steaks
Festive holiday scenes with snow flakes
But when Route 66
No longer had kicks
The reindeer gave way to the snakes

CHRISTMAS ISLAND, AUSTRALIA

For this Christmas segment of our holiday chapter we're going to take you on a trip to Christmas Island and do some fact checking on the lyrics of the classic song. By the end of this you're going to be able to make an informed decision as to whether you really would like to spend Christmas there, or not. We love the story of this island.

Christmas Island is an Australian territory located in the Indian Ocean about halfway between India and Australia. A full 63% of the 52-square-mile island is dedicated to a national park and the diverse topography features everything from a rain forest to wetlands to waterfalls. A unique array of flora and fauna populate the island along with about 1,600 people. The island is ringed with snorkeling and diving reefs.

LAST INHABITED PLACE ON EARTH ~ One significant contributing factor as to why Christmas Island turned out to be such a beautiful and unique place is that it was literally the last habitable island in the world to become inhabited. When Britain claimed the island in 1887, there was not a soul on it. In 1897 they began to plot a strategy for the development of the island. Step one in this process was that an expedition, led by Charles Andrews, spent ten months on the island from mid-1897 to mid-1898.

The bottom line was that they thought things through before settling and developing the island and took the time to do it right. The expedition produced a 359-page volume documenting the island's flora, fauna, and geographical features.

In his introduction, Andrews stated his mission as follows: "It seemed highly desirable that this interesting island should be carefully examined and described by a competent naturalist and geologist before being opened up by Europeans for agricultural and commercial purposes in that it is the only existing island never inhabited by man, savage or civilized."

Another way of restating Andrews' summary would be to say that of any piece of land on the planet where people actually live today, Christmas Island was the last place to become inhabited. So on the whole, Christmas Island is blessed with a nice combination of natural beauty and personal planning.

THE SONG "CHRISTMAS ISLAND" ~ Next let's apply the theorem of the plausible impossible to fact check some of the lyrics of the "Christmas Island" song. Most of the lyrics are fairly generic and don't lend themselves to the concept of fact checking, but here are the ones that do.

"Let's get away from sleigh bells, let's get away from snow."
There's no law against sleigh bells, so some troublemaker could conceivably smuggle some of those in, but the escape from snow is a sure thing. The temperature never drops below 60° on Christmas Island.

"How'd ya like to hang your stocking on a great big coconut tree?"
This would be easy, those trees are all over the damn place.

"How'd ya like to stay up late, like the islanders do?"
Well, you may be staying up by yourself. The island is not known for late night partying.

"Wait for Santa to sail in with your presents in a canoe."
Even if you are a true believer, this one's probably not gonna happen. In all likelihood Santa will be taking the sleigh on this run due to logistical circumstances. The closest possible location from which Santa could launch his canoe would be 310 miles away at the southwestern tip of Indonesia. In order for this to actually happen Santa would probably have to start paddling shortly after Thanksgiving, clearly shirking his many pre-holiday obligations.

"For every day your Christmas dreams come true."
Our take on this would be that if you could snap your fingers and be there it sounds like a tropical paradise with a tantalizing appeal. But the logistics certainly present a challenge; the only flights in emanate from Australia. So for most of us, we may just have to rely on the magic of Christmas and see if we can hitch a ride in on Santa's sleigh.

CHRISTMAS PIE, ENGLAND

This tasty hamlet is located in southeast England and is home for a few hundred. In the 17th century most of the land in town was owned by two families bearing the somewhat unusual surnames of Christmas and Pie. When the two families merged their farmland to form a larger more efficient operation, the two last names coalesced and the community became known as Christmas Pie. We'd like a piece with whipped cream.

CHAPTER 22
THE WILD WILD WEST

You better be **Rough and Ready** because this one's a real shoot 'em up. We will share with you the stories of how **Death Valley** got its name and what really happened with the Shootout at the O.K. Corral in **Tombstone**. We'll muddle some myths that have prevailed as most people's go-to take on how things went down at the most famous gun fight in the history of the Old West. Wyatt Earp was not the leader of the good guys and the gunfight did not occur at the O.K. Corral.

TOMBSTONE, ARIZONA

In the 1870's when prospector Edward Schieffelin expressed to soldiers his interest in mining this part of southeast Arizona, he was told that the only thing he would find was his own tombstone (plus some Indians). Well the soldiers were off by a bit. Schieffelin discovered rich veins of silver in Tombstone, and the town went on to become one of the West's wealthiest, as well as most lawless.

The town was the site of the Shootout at the O.K. Corral, probably the most famous gunfight in the history of the American West. Here's a quick overview of the chaos at the corral. There were nine primary participants, four on the side of the law and five outside the law. The starting lineup for the "good guys" consisted of Doc Holliday, and the Earp brothers Virgil, Morgan, and Wyatt. The "bad guys" were the Clanton brothers Ike and Billy, the McLaury brothers, Tom and Frank, and Billy Claiborne.

The whole thing went down in a hurry at about 3:00 p.m. on Wednesday, October 26, 1881. The entire shootout lasted just 30 seconds with about 30 shots fired and the good guys prevailing. Billy Clanton and both McLaury brothers were killed while Ike Clanton and Billy Claiborne took off and ran. Virgil, Morgan, and Doc Holliday were wounded, but Wyatt Earp was unharmed.

Right now we'll bust two myths about this historical event. First, Wyatt Earp is often erroneously regarded as the central figure in the shootout, although his brother Virgil was Tombstone city marshal and U.S. deputy marshal that day and Virgil had far more experience as a lawman than Wyatt.

Second, the shootout did not take place at the O.K. Corral, an establishment whose rear entrance was actually six doors west of the fight. So where did the fight occur? It happened in front of C. S. Fly's Photo Studio.

It was actually the 1946 movie that cemented both of the aforementioned myths in many minds. That film was based on the biography of Wyatt Earp so it tended to spin things so as to emphasize his importance. And in terms of the title, *Shootout at C.S. Fly's Photo Studio* just doesn't quite have the same allure of frontier adventure as *Shootout at the O.K. Corral*, now does it?

> *We cross our hearts and hope to die*
> *The O.K. Corral was a lie*
> *And you can't tip your hat*
> *To the bad Shootout at*
> *The Photo Shop of C.S. Fly*

DEATH VALLEY, CALIFORNIA

This place received its ominous designation from a group of pioneers lost there in the winter of 1849-1850. Only one of the "Lost '49ers" actually died there, but they all assumed they would. According to the National Park Service, the naming happened like this: "As the party climbed out of the valley over the Panamint Mountains, one of the men turned, looked back, and said 'goodbye, Death Valley.'"

While this is the specific incident to which the naming of the valley is attributed, only one life was lost in that particular group. That being said, many others did die in Death Valley. The valley became a thoroughfare of sorts because of the California Gold Rush.

For prospectors heading to California from the southwest it was the most direct route to their destination.

So how many people died in Death Valley? During the Gold Rush era the single most deadly event occurred when one wagon train expedition suffered thirteen deaths in traversing the valley. And of course there have been occasional deaths there ever since. Over the past 15 years there have been twelve heat-related fatalities.

Next question… do any people actually live in Death Valley? The answer to this would be a qualified, "yes." The people who live there are the people who work there. Death Valley features three permanent tourist sites which attract 1.2 million guests per year and some of the people who staff those sites have accommodations in the valley.

The highest recorded air temperature on the surface of the earth was recorded in Death Valley on the afternoon of July 10, 1913. On that day the mercury soared to 134° F, so if you're planning to add yourself to the ranks of those million tourists taking in Death Valley, make sure the air conditioning is working before you head in.

ROUGH AND READY, CALIFORNIA

Ironically these were the first two boxes we checked on the dating app that initiated our relationship. Actually not. In case you skipped the introduction, we met in high school before anybody even had a computer. But here's the story behind this Rough and Ready town of about a thousand people which is located in northeastern California, 62 miles east of Sacramento.

The first established settlement in Rough and Ready was made in the fall of 1849 by a mining company from Wisconsin, known as the Rough and Ready Company, during the California Gold Rush. The company's leader, Captain A. A. Townsend, named the company after General Zachary Taylor (nicknamed "Old Rough and Ready"), who had been elected as the 12th president of the United States that year. That nickname had been bestowed upon Taylor for his reputation as a fearless military leader during the Mexican American War, during which Townsend served under Taylor.

Things took on a rather ironic twist fairly early in the game. Allegiance to the president notwithstanding, the town declared its secession from the Union, and declared independence as The Great Republic of Rough and Ready on April 7, 1850, largely to avoid federal mining taxes. Seemed like a good idea at the time, but not so fast. Three months later some of the townspeople went to Nevada City to purchase booze for their 4th of July celebration and were not allowed to do so because they were "foreigners."

So at this point it became a battle of principles and there were basically two choices. Which principle was more important to the folks of Rough and Ready?

- No Taxation without representation
- Intoxication is worth the taxation

The decision was, "Let's all do a shot and pay the damn taxes." In order to celebrate Independence Day in staggering style, Rough and Ready rejoined the Union on the 4th of July 1850, less than three months after seceding. It remained a thriving community for over a hundred years.

The end of the trail essentially came for Rough and Ready in the mid-1980's when the new State Route 20 bypassed the town. While there are still about a thousand people living within the town limits, the old downtown commercial section is pretty much shuttered.

We found an interview with a lady named Jayna Ashcraft who has lived in Rough and Ready with her husband for 25 years now. Putting the town in modern-day perspective she said, "We're pretty much just a novelty at this point. When I tell people where I live, they sometimes don't believe me. When I've ordered stuff from different companies, they call back to double-check, making sure that the address is, in fact, Rough and Ready."

Summarizing the rest of the interview, there was further justification for companies double checking the accuracy of the Ashcraft address. The couple lives on "To Hell and Back Lane." Honest to God.

CHAPTER 23
YOU'RE KILLING US

Well, we've got bad news and more bad news. In this chapter you're going to die and in the following chapter you're going to go to Hell. If it softens the blow, we'll go with you. But before we put you on that hellbound train, let's cover the prerequisite. We will take you from **Deadhorse**, Alaska to **Dead Horse Bay,** New York. We can wax poetic and check out all the **Fresh Kills** at **Kill Devil Hills**. And if you're up for it after that, we can drive our woody to **Slaughter Beach**, where the surf is never up.

This chapter comes hell or high water
Delaware's got a beach that's called Slaughter
We'll hit Deadhorse too
And chart our course to
Dead Horse Bay where we won't drink the water

KILL DEVIL HILLS, NORTH CAROLINA

The North Carolina license plates proudly proclaim "First in Flight" and in this segment we are going to bust a related myth. When asked where Orville and Wilbur Wright flew the first airplane, everyone knows it was Kitty Hawk. Wright? Well, that's not right. And we'll explain why in this entry.

Kill Devil Hills is a town on the Outer Banks of North Carolina. It is home to the Wright Brothers National Memorial and about 7,000 people. Here's the scoop on the name.

During the 1700's, rum smugglers were active on the coast of Carolina. Some of the rum was rather robust. How powerful was it? The locals said the rum was strong enough to "kill the devil." Combine that with the preponderance of sand dunes that line the Outer Banks, shake it all up, and out pours Kill Devil Hills.

The town is home to the site of the Wright Brothers' first successful motor-operated airplane flights on December 17, 1903. So, why has

Kitty Hawk lapped up all the glory for all that time since? The explanation is actually pretty straight forward and sensible.

The town of Kill Devil Hills did not officially incorporate until 1953, so fifty years prior to that when the Wright Brothers first flew, the closest population center that was actually a place was Kitty Hawk, four miles to the north. So we are pleased to give Kill Devil Hills its proper due, and do remember, time flies when you're having rum.

DEADHORSE, ALASKA

Deadhorse is more of a work camp than a town in the traditional sense. It was established to support oil development in the surrounding area. Most buildings are modular, pre-fabricated types, situated on gravel pads on the tundra bog. Virtually all the businesses are engaged in oil field or pipeline support such as drilling, construction and maintenance.

If you ever found yourself in Anchorage, the largest city in Alaska, you'd probably be thinking you're pretty far north, correct? Well, if you were in Anchorage, you'd have to travel 853 miles north to get to Deadhorse. Most folks who make this trip are doing so because they work at the nearby Prudhoe Bay Oil Field. Your other travel option would be to fly into Deadhorse Airport.

The permanent population is variously listed as being between 25 and 50 residents. Temporary residents (employed by various oil companies) can range as high as 3,000. Deadhorse is way up there, located on the north coast of Alaska. Just to share some stats with you, it's 250 miles north of the Arctic Circle and 1,200 miles south of the North Pole. This location results in some unusual lengths of night and day as indicated in the list below.

- Longest day: 63 days, 23 hours, 40 minutes (12:09 a.m. on May 20 to 11:18 p.m. on July 22)
- Shortest day: 45 min (11:42 a.m. to 12:27 p.m. on November 24)
- Longest night: 54 days, 22 hours, 51 min (12:27 p.m. on November 24 to 11:18 a.m. on January 18)

- Shortest night: 26 min (11:43 p.m. on May 19 to 12:09 a.m. on May 20)
- Highest recorded temperature: 85°F on July 13, 2016
- Lowest recorded temperature: –62°F on January 27, 1989
- The coldest recorded wind chill: –102°F on January 28, 1989

During the summer there is a modicum of tourism. Visitors can arrange to visit the Arctic Ocean via a guided tour only. There is no longer any public Arctic Ocean access from Deadhorse. All tours must be booked 24 hours in advance to allow time for background checks on all passengers going through the oilfield checkpoint.

Arctic wildlife is prevalent in the area. Indigenous species include Arctic foxes, Arctic ground squirrels, grizzly bears, polar bears, musk oxen, and Arctic hares. The area often features large herds of caribou and over 200 bird and waterfowl species, including geese, swans, gulls and eagles.

Tourists traveling to Deadhorse typically take tour buses from Fairbanks via the Dalton Highway, a two-day journey with an overnight stop in Coldfoot. During the summer months, tourists can also experience the midnight sun due to Deadhorse's location above the Arctic Circle. Because alcoholic beverages are not sold in Deadhorse, a humorous slogan for the town is "All that far and still no bar." So if you think you're going to need a belt to make it through your Deadhorse vacation remember to BYOB.

If you happen to be a motorcycle enthusiast we've got the perfect excuse for you to visit Deadhorse. The town is the culmination of the Iron Butt Association motorcycle rider challenge billed as "The Ultimate Coast to Coast." This ride starts from Key West, Florida, and gives riders 30 days to reach Deadhorse.

The settlement dates back to the 1967 discovery of the Prudhoe Bay oil field. The origin of the quirky name is that it refers to the original airfield runway, which was built with gravel hauled by the Deadhorse Hauling trucking company. This of course begs the question of how the trucking company was named. Turns out the owner decided to name his company after the most bizarre job it ever landed. One summer they signed a contract to haul away dead horses in Fairbanks. Tough job but somebody has to do it.

SLAUGHTER BEACH, DELAWARE

Slaughter Beach is a small town with just a few hundred permanent residents, but the population does swell during the summer tourist season. It is located on the Delaware Bay in the southern part of the state.

The name itself warrants an almost oxymoronic take, doesn't it? The "Beach" image tends to send out "Good Vibrations," but egads, what about the "Slaughter?" That is a pointed and intriguing question. And the next thing we're going to do is add to the intrigue.

One of the concepts that we found so compelling when we first started to delve into this topic of quirky place names was the frequency with which multiple theories would surface regarding their origins. Amidst this mayhem, Slaughter Beach emerges not only as an oxymoron, it comes in at #1 on our list of places which had the most potential theories in the mix as to where the name emanated from. We have five for you.

Theory #1 ~ It was named after William Slaughter, the first postmaster for this locality who served in the mid-19th century.

Theory #2 ~ In the spring and early summer, swarms of horseshoe crabs crawl ashore to spawn. The wave action of low tide flips some of the crabs over leaving them to die, thus the "Slaughter of the Crabs."

Theory #3 ~ A local legend tells of a man named Brabant who, in the mid-18th century, killed several Native Americans with a cannon in order to fend off an impending attack. According to the legend, the Indians were lured in by being told the cannon was a "God" who would bring peace. Herein lies your "Slaughter of the Indians" theory.

Theory #4 ~ Early maps show a small creek named Slaughter Creek, which flowed through the area and emptied into the Delaware Bay, just north of Slaughter Beach.

Theory #5 ~ Just to the southwest of the town is an area called "Slaughter Neck." Geographically speaking, a "neck" is a marshy land strip connecting two larger areas of dry land.

There's one worldwide organization which is overdue for an appearance in our book, and for better or worse, they're back. The last time we heard from PETA was in Chapter 2 when those merry pranksters were in Tasmania trying to convince the town of Eggs and Bacon Bay to change their name to Apples & Cherries Bay.

We truly hope you will all appreciate the animal analogy we'll apply in this next sentence. After being informed that the name of Eggs & Bacon Bay was based upon an indigenous flower which blossomed egg-yellow and bacon-red, PETA had no choice but to go home from that one with their tails between their legs.

That Tasmanian mission having gone "a-fowl" in 2016, PETA sat on its haunches in the town "name game" until 2018. Clearly putting all of their eggs in theory basket #2 from the previous page, the one based upon the dying crabs, PETA approached the Town of Slaughter Beach with a request.

PETA asked that the town change its name from "Slaughter Beach" to "Sanctuary Beach." In an attempt to sweeten the proposition, PETA offered to pay for new signage if the name was adopted. From Tasmania to Delaware, PETA has had to travel literally from one side of the globe to the other to learn that convincing towns to change historic names because some vague animal offense might be implied is an idea that is simply not going to fly.

DEAD HORSE BAY, NEW YORK

This gets our award for the most dismal description of the chapter. Dead Horse Bay was named in the mid-19th century for the dozens of dead horse processing plants that lined the beach, where the carcasses of New York City carriage horses and other animals were manufactured into glue.

Today chopped-up chunks of weathered horse bones still wash up on the beach, which is also covered in shards of glass bottles and china, cosmetics containers, and children's toys, all dating back to when the area also served as a garbage dump. This place is a chocolate mess.

FRESH KILLS, NEW YORK

Fresh Kills is a 3.5 square mile parcel of land in the New York City borough of Staten Island. It comes with a "That Was Then, This is Now" storyline. Let's summarize and then we'll circle back and provide some details. It was once the largest landfill in the world and currently it is undergoing a long gradual process of being reinvented as a park.

The name sounds like something that could have been assigned to the landfill to reflect the negative connotations associated with tens of thousands of tons of garbage. That however is not the case as before the landfill was established, the Fresh Kills moniker was already in use as the name of the estuary body of water found on the western shore of Staten Island.

Fresh Kills opened in 1948 as a temporary landfill, supposedly with a life span of three years or less. Perhaps not surprisingly, that plan fell by the wayside and by 1955 it had become the largest landfill in the world, and remained so until its closure in 2001.

At the peak of its operation, in 1986, Fresh Kills received 29,000 tons of residential waste per day. From 1991 until its closing it was the only landfill accepting New York City's waste.

We found lots of descriptions about how unsavory the site was and, to share one example with you folks, we are deferring to the words of Samuel Kearing, who served as sanitation commissioner under New York Mayor John V. Lindsay. Here is what he had to say about his first visit to Fresh Kills in 1970.

"It had a certain nightmare quality... I can still recall looking down on the operation from a control tower and thinking that Fresh Kills had for thousands of years been a magnificent, teeming, literally life-enhancing tidal marsh. And in just twenty-five years, it was gone, buried under millions of tons of New York City's refuse.

Animals were also a problem. Feral dog packs roamed the dump and were a hazard to employees. Rats also posed a problem. Attempts to suppress the population with poison failed."

As a result of intense community pressure and, with the support of New York Mayor Rudy Giuliani and Governor George Pataki, a state law was passed in 1996 requiring that the landfill cease accepting solid waste by the end of 2001. By 1997, two of the four landfill mounds were closed and covered with a thick, impermeable cap. The landfill closed forever and received its last barge of garbage on March 22, 2001. Sort of.

So in the history of New York City when does "closed forever" not mean "closed forever?" The answer to that question would be "in the aftermath of 9/11."

After the September 11, 2001 attacks, Fresh Kills was temporarily re-opened to be used as a sorting ground for roughly one-third of the rubble from Ground Zero. About 1.6 million tons of material obtained from Ground Zero was taken to the landfill for sorting.

Thousands of detectives and forensic evidence specialists worked for over 1.7 million hours at the Fresh Kills Landfill to try to sort and recover remnants of the people killed in the attacks, as well as their possessions. More than 1,600 personal effects and 4,257 human remains were retrieved during this time, but only 300 people were identified.

In October 2008, reclamation of the site began for a multi-phase, 30-year redevelopment plan. The goal is for the landfill to be turned into Freshkills Park. The rationale for changing Fresh Kills to Freshkills was so that the word "Kills" doesn't scream at you as intensely.

At a size of 3.5 square miles Freshkills Park will be three times the size of Central Park. It will consist of a variety of public spaces and facilities for multiple types of activities. The site is large enough to support many sports and programs including nature trails, horseback riding, mountain biking, community events, outdoor dining, sports fields, and canoeing/kayaking. While the park project won't be completed until 2037, parts of it have already opened.

DEADWOOD, SOUTH DAKOTA

"There's gold in them thar hills," were the words uttered in the southwest corner of South Dakota when gold was discovered in the Black Hills in 1874. Of the several towns that spontaneously sprung up in the aftermath of the gold rush, none would go on to achieve the level of fame of Deadwood, South Dakota.

The person to whom the above quote could be attributed would actually be General George Custer. It was he who led an expedition into the Black Hills and announced the discovery of gold in 1874 on French Creek near present-day Custer, South Dakota. While several towns spontaneously sprang into existence, for whatever reasons the most notorious of the outlaws, gamblers and gunslingers who headed for the Dakota Territory drifted into Deadwood.

Non-existent at the beginning of 1874, the population of Deadwood had reached 5,000 by 1875 and peaked at 25,000 the following year. Amongst those joining the party were the trigger-happy Calamity Jane, Potato Creek Johnny, Wyatt Earp, Seth Bullock, and Wild Bill Hickok.

Calamity Jane was a frontierswoman known for her marksmanship and daredevil ways, as well as being an acquaintance of Wild Bill Hickok's. She accompanied him not only in life but also in death. The pair are buried side-by-side in the Deadwood Cemetery. While Jane died of pneumonia at the age of 51, Wild Bill's demise was much more sudden and it went down in Deadwood.

On August 2, 1886 at Nuttal & Mann's Saloon, Wild Bill Hickok was playing poker in a game including Jack McCall. After losing badly, McCall left the table angry at Hickok despite Hickok's offer to help him pay his debt. He returned later and shot Hickok in the back of the head at point blank range.

Hickok died instantly and McCall was later hung for murder. One aspect of this event has lived in infamy. At the time of his death, Hickok was holding a poker hand of black aces and eights, known forever after as the "Dead Man's Hand."

With Calamity Jane by his side
It was Deadwood where Wild Bill died
We'll visit Fresh Kills
And then Kill Devil Hills
Where the Wright brothers turned glide to flied

Nowadays, Deadwood keeps its loud and lusty heritage alive with a wealth of Wild West-inspired attractions, from museums and parades to lively Vegas-style casinos.

Chapter 24
Go to Hell

Because you know how much we love to take care of you, we're awarding you the following bonus. We are actually going to take you to **Hell** twice. There's one in Michigan and one in Norway. What will it be like when we get there? Not surprisingly it's going to be **Hotazel**, which can be found in South Africa. There were only two place names that came up three times in our book. The first was Santa Claus back in Chapter 20 and the second is **Satan's Kingdom** which can be found in the states of Connecticut, Massachusetts and Vermont.

Here's a little bit of irony for you; did you ever realize that Satan and Santa are anagrams? Well, the fact that we spend time thinking about things like that is probably the reason that we're going to **Hell For Certain** (which is in Kentucky).

HELL, NORWAY

Hell is a sleepy post town with a train station, grocery store, restaurant, gas station and of course, a retirement home, in case a retirement in Hell sounds like a better idea than Florida. The town of 1,600 is one of the colder places in the world and in fact, Hell literally freezes over for about a third of the year.

In terms of etymology, the founders of this burg in southwestern Norway named it "Hell" after the Old Norse word "hellir,"" which translates to "overhang." Not to the extent of Hell, Michigan, which we'll cover later in this chapter, but Hell, Norway does have some fun with its name and there are definitely attempts to capitalize upon it.

Because of its uniquely classic Norwegian architecture, the train station provides the most frequented photo opportunity for those who enjoy having permanent visual documentation of the fact that they've literally been to Hell and back. Trondheim is the nearest city and when you land at the airport there, Facebook gives you the option to indicate your location as having "just landed in Hell."

Several commercial entities between Hell and Trondheim employ the devilish title even though they are not actually in the town. Sure, you could call yourself the Sandfærhus Shopping Center, but it just doesn't have quite the same ring as the Shopping Center From Hell, does it?

Hell was put on the map, figuratively speaking, in 1990 when hometown gal Mona Grudt, a green-eyed redhead, was the Norway's Miss Universe representative. While billing yourself as "the beauty queen from Hell" might not seem like the best strategy, Grudt actually became the only Norwegian girl to ascend the throne and become Miss Universe. She subsequently parlayed that achievement into an extremely successful Norwegian TV career with several of her appearances available on YouTube.

HELL FOR CERTAIN, KENTUCKY

Folks in this rural community in southeastern Kentucky like this name so much they used it twice. The town is located on Hell For Certain Creek which bisects the town. The name came from an incident when an early attempt to establish a church there was rebuffed. The minister returned to church headquarters and on their state map of Kentucky labeled the spot "Hell For Certain."

Later efforts to bring that old time religion to this rural outpost succeeded and currently written above the entry to the church is the phrase, "The greatest people in the world walk through these doors every Sunday." Looks like the folks from Hell For Certain are going to Heaven For Sure.

HOTAZEL, SOUTH AFRICA

Welcome to Hotazel, where it's hot as hell– or at least it was on the day in 1915 when a group of land surveyors assessed a farm in South Africa and named the whole place "Hot As Hell." Over time the spelling morphed to "Hotazel" but the pronunciation remains unaltered.

Hotazel is located in the northwest corner of South Africa and boasts a population of about 1,000. Ironically, the climate is actually pretty reasonable, with summer temperatures sometimes reaching the 90's and winter temperatures sometimes dipping into the 30's. On some of those winter nights natives have been heard uttering the ironic comment, "Tonight it's Coldazel in Hotazel!"

SATAN'S KINGDOM, MASSACHUSETTS

The name of this community seems to stem from a combination of two factors. When settlers first came into the area in the 1670's they were fiercely repelled by the indigenous Native Americans. Once the settlers did establish themselves, the rough terrain and wildlife of Satan's Kingdom made life difficult for the colonists.

This small village is in the northern part of Massachusetts, near the Vermont border. That location is a bit ironic because there are exactly three towns in the U.S. named Satan's Kingdom and one of the other two is in Vermont. We'll take you there next.

SATAN'S KINGDOM, VERMONT

This town in the northwest corner of the state is apparently not a farmers' heaven. Our volume of information on this one is thin. There was a woman named Esther Munroe Swift who published a book in 1977 called *Vermont Place-Names: Footprints of History*. In this book her stated goal was to cover every conceivable place name in Vermont.

In a side note, we came to the conclusion that Swift's book must not have been a big seller. We went to Amazon to check out background info on this publication and the cheapest copy available was a used one going for $900. A lot of the time people's initial reactions to a figure like this is the opposite of what it should be. Your instinctive reaction to seeing that price might be, "This must have been great!"

Your actual reaction should be, "This must have really sucked!" Why you ask? It all boils down to supply and demand. If a book sells a million copies, there's going to be hundreds of thousands of used ones drifting back into the secondary market. A book coming out and selling next to nothing provides the scenario where, if years later, it becomes desirable for some reason, the price has the potential to go sky high because there are very few copies in existence.

Obviously there are not many copies of *Vermont Place-Names: Footprints of History* by Esther Munroe Swift out there. So before we get back to Satan's Kingdom, let us just share the following. If you lived in Vermont in the late 1970's, and could have easily scarfed up a few dozen of these at $9.95 each, you should really be kicking yourself in the ass right now. If you do the math, a two dozen box of these babies would be worth $216,000 today.

At any rate, Swift's one line about Satan's Kingdom was that it was "thought to have been named by someone who had expected fertile, rolling acres and had received rocks and hills instead." Satan's Kingdom was apparently named because its rocky soil was unsuitable for farming.

At this point, we are going to excuse all of our readers from Vermont who we know are heading directly to the attic to check that old box of books your parents passed down to you.

SATAN'S KINGDOM, CONNECTICUT

Our research revealed some overlapping theories on how this community came to be known as Satan's Kingdom. These theories generally coalesce around a common theme so here's our composite storyline. Also there's one touchy element of the story that we'll deal with right now and be done with it. The story has some overtones of racism which, let's face it, are part of our history. By no means do we intend to condone this; we're just writers researching history.

In general, the area was plagued by rocky, unfertile soil, which made it not conducive for farming, therefore it was not a place a lot of people wanted to go. So who ended up with no other options but resort to the forbidding wilds of Satan's Kingdom? It was basically a collection of society's outcasts who had been rejected from more desirable locations.

There were Native Americans who had been expelled from their respective tribes. There were African Americans who were runaway slaves and/or people who didn't fit in to more mainstream black communities. And there were renegade whites who weren't accepted elsewhere. For lack of a kinder description, Satan's Kingdom was basically a melting pot for undesirables. It was a haven for thieves, robbers and outlaws to hideout and launch their exploits of criminal mischief.

These days Satan's Kingdom is a tranquil and scenic recreation area which hosts a huge business facilitating tubing down the Farmington River in the summer. As we've seen become a frequent problem for communities with unusual names, the Satan's Kingdom Road sign was repeatedly being targeted for theft. What self-respecting, head-banging, pot-smoking teenage stoner wouldn't want to hang one of those satanic salutes in his bedroom?

So while we've seen this problem before, we truly love how this Connecticut community chose to deal with it. They came up with the ingenious idea of intentionally misspelling the name on the sign to decrease the desirability of theft! We'd love to see the hidden camera footage of the hoodlum mentioned in the previous paragraph when he gets home from his successful sign stealing stunt and fires up a fat doobie to celebrate.

Then upon hanging up his new street sign right above his Ozzy Osbourne poster, imagine the double take when he realizes he's stolen the sign for "STATAN'S KINGDOM." Talk about your ultimate buzzkill! And of course there would be that priceless period of prolonged purgatory when the poor kid is wondering, "Is that sign actually misspelled or am I just really high?!"

Satan's Kingdoms' signs they all said "Satan's"
With sign theft they did lose their patience
Sober plan by the owners
To perplex the stoners
Let's misspell the sign to say "Statan's"

HELL, MICHIGAN

As we've taken you on our tour of fanciful place names, this is one of the few that has taken its quirky name, run with it, and managed to turn itself into a full-fledged tourist attraction. Hell is located in the southeastern part of the state, 15 miles northwest of Ann Arbor, which is the home of the University of Michigan. And there is definitely kind of a college-town vibe burning in Hell.

The town officially adopted the name in 1841 with three competing theories as to the etymology. We'll go from least fun to most fun in our review of the possibilities here.

Theory #1 ~ The name came from a pair of Germans visiting in the 1830's who described the town as "so schön hell" ("so beautifully bright").

Theory #2 ~ This theory concerns town founder George Reeves, who, when asked for an opinion on naming the new town, supposedly replied, "I don't know, you can name it Hell for all I care."

Theory #3 ~ Another theory states that Reeves, who owned a general store and grist mill, was known to pay farmhands in whiskey, prompting their wives to complain that their husbands had "gone to Hell again," when they failed to turn up for supper.

At any rate, the locals have enthusiastically embraced the name, playing up every opportunity to turn both municipal and commercial signage and advertising into a pun connoisseur's dream come true. Visit during winter to see "Hell freeze over," or stop by the Heluva Good Deal Auto-Mart.

The town has implemented a variety of kitschy activities and unusual gifts and knickknacks making use of the town's name. The establishment that is the base of operations for many of the activities is *Screams Souvenirs from Hell and Helloween* which is located on Hell's main drag of Patterson Lake Road. At *Screams* it is possible to make arrangements to get married, become Mayor for the day, or literally become the legal owner of your own little piece of Hell. What the devil more could you ask for?

We'll save that trifecta of opportunities for last and start off by sharing with you some of the other hellish options available. The specialty of the Creamatory ice cream shop at *Screams* is the Gravedigger Sundae. If you can devour the whole thing, they will not assume any responsibility for your demise, but they will sign, seal, and singe (as opposed to sign) your Death Certificate.

You can visit the Hell Hole Diner "where the pastries are to die for." Another dining option is the Hell Saloon where you can "bring your family for a little Hell on Earth." Damnation University has a hundred different types of degrees and you can get your Damn U diploma at *Screams*.

Another idea which we found rather novel was the Locks of Love Bridge. It's a 35-foot-long bridge with lots of lattice work to support the premise. We'll start with the nutshell summary of how it works. At *Screams* any couple can buy their personal lock and key. Then you go to the bridge and symbolically lock in your love and throw away the key.

Upon arrival at the Locks of Love Bridge the couple can pick any piece of available lattice work to which they can attach their lock and throw away the key into the Hell Creek River which flows underneath the bridge. Once your key to love is down there, you can pretty much rest assured that the world would have to go to Hell in a handbasket before that love would die.

LAND OWNER IN HELL ~ Of the "Big 3" opportunities we mentioned above, this one comes in at the bargain price of $9.99. For less than ten bucks you can leave town with the official land title to one square inch of prime property in Hell and membership in the Hell Landowner's Society. Bonus notes: the titles are all singed (burned) free of charge and you can buy land in Hell through their website.

This actually might make a nice gift for the person who has everything. Next Christmas they open their gift envelope to find their singed certificate along with whatever "Hell" cliché best suits your collective personalities. A couple possibilities might be "I've been to Hell and back for you." or "To a Hell of a guy/gal." Obviously there are many more.

MAYOR FOR A DAY ~ This one needs to be arranged online in advance. For a paltry payment of $100 you can become the Mayor of Hell for a day. The perks will pull you from Purgatory. You can visit Hell's website for complete details but here are some highlights.

In addition to the official key to the city, the Mayor of Hell receives a set of devil horns to wear, a coffee mug, badge, wallet card, bottle of Hell dirt, and the one square inch of property described in the entry above. The mayor also receives phone calls throughout the day for tasks and decisions.

Additionally, the mayor is awarded a t-shirt with "Mayor of Hell" on the front and "impeached" on the back. This job comes with the pre-ordained guarantee that you will be ignominiously impeached at the end of the day in order to vacate the spot for the next day's mayor. If you are interested in pursuing the mayor gig, sign up early because the dates book fast.

MARRIAGE IN HELL ~ While this option may seem repulsively unromantic, there are certainly upsides. Take for example the slogan emblazoned upon the church in Hell. The sobering saying reads, "After all, a marriage that starts in Hell has no place to go but up." Well, that's certainly one way of looking at it.

Okay, now let's talk finances and logistics. They have hosted hundreds of weddings in Hell so this is not some amateurish ordeal where you leave wondering if you're really married. Hell's Chapel of Love is both quaint and fun, from the question mark on the top of the steeple, to the blue doors meant to ward off evil spirits. The chapel itself holds a dozen guests including the couple and officiant, but their park-like grounds can accommodate an outdoor ceremony of up to 150 guests.

Hell's Chapel of Love and surrounding grounds can be rented by the hour. The cost is $125 for the first hour and $100 per additional hour. This also includes a reading of your wedding proclamation in Hell, Michigan, two complimentary wine glasses, and a special United in Hell magnet. This does not include the officiant, legal marriage license, catering, bar services, rental equipment, etc. Those are additional and arranged separately by the wedding party.

In Michigan's Hell you can say
I own land and it's my wedding day
And just to convey that
You will be the fat cat
You're Mayor of Hell for the day

So there's your overview of Hell, Michigan. It is a very festive creative place where a lot of thought has gone into numerous clever ways to play upon the satanic title of the town. Devilish fun has begun! So, if the whole shebang sounds like a shindig sure to satisfy, you can get all fired up and go to Hell!

ADDENDUM #1
OUR *WHAT'S IN A NAME?* TOP 25

After we finished our initial draft of this book, we picked 15 friends to read it through and share any thoughts or questions they might have. Since we were doing that anyway, we came up with the idea of closing this book with a Top 25 and we asked our readers to tell us their favorite 5-to-10 stories within the book. Once the votes were in, we tallied them up and what you see below are the results. Feel free to compare them to your own ballot.

25 ~ SHITTERTON, ENGLAND ~ Well, the name means pretty much just what it sounds like. When that moniker evolved over a thousand years ago, it was a reflection of the fact that the town was located on an open sewer. But it's not a town without honor. The Find My Past genealogy website named Shitterton #1 in its list of Britain's Worst Place Names. A highlight of this story is that they came up with our second favorite method to prevent people from sign stealing, which is a common problem for towns with intriguing names like this.

24 ~ VERY STUPID, FRANCE ~ Mayor Georges Leherle is on record as saying that, "Despite the name of our town, we're no stupider than anyone else." Believe it or not, there is actually an Association of French Villages with Funny Names. And, pardon our French, what we found very stupid was that Very Stupid was the 39th town adopted into the association. How 'bout the list of #1-38!

23 ~ SEXMOAN, PHILIPPINES ~ And the punch line is… this place was named by Spanish friars. We're assuming that the Spanish holy men who bestowed the name had never even had sex, let alone moaned about it. They were most likely oblivious to any kind of English translation which might take on sexual connotations. This was one of a handful of towns that put the concept of changing its controversial name up to a vote.

22 ~ CHRISTMAS ISLAND, AUSTRALIA ~ This is clearly one of the most unique places on Earth and we have a very solid justification for making the statement. Of any inhabitable island on the planet, Christmas Island was literally the last one to become inhabited. Before the British allowed anybody in, extensive research and planning was completed with a goal of creating a utopian environment. And then of course there's the killer Christmas song for which we do an accuracy analysis of the lyrics.

21 ~ DEADWOOD, SOUTH DAKOTA ~ If you're a poker player, you're familiar with the phrase of a "Dead Man's Hand" which includes black aces and eights. That evil lexicon entered the English language in Deadwood. That was the hand Wild Bill Hickok was holding on August 2, 1886 at Nuttal & Mann's Saloon when Jack McCall shot him in the back of the head at point blank range. McCall was subsequently hung and Hickok currently lies in his grave next to Calamity Jane in the Deadwood Cemetery.

20 ~ VAGINA, RUSSIA ~ Okay, we know this is one you're going to want to delve deeply into. As you've seen in our book, the concept of foreign countries, which speak different languages, long ago adopting names that coincidentally had risqué meanings in English is not unusual. This storyline stood out because the rebellious Russians of this village actually changed their name **from** Kolkhoz **to** Vagina in 1991.

19 ~ TOMBSTONE, ARIZONA ~ This town got its name when founder Edward Schieffelin was told all he'd find there was a bunch of Indians and his grave. Well, the silver lining of this would be that mineral was exactly what he found. Deep veins of silver waiting to be mined led to an influx of people, lawlessness and lies. The Shootout at the O.K. Corral was not led by Wyatt Earp and did not happen at the O.K. Corral. But the Shootout at C.S. Fly's Photo Studio just doesn't quite have the same allure of frontier adventure as the Shootout at the O.K. Corral, now, does it?

18 ~ KNOCKEMSTIFF, OHIO ~ This was pointed out as being one of the more poignant passages we penned, with the pessimism being palpable. It's a collection of stories linked by violence, alcoholism and drug abuse. One character actually swigs Old Grand Dad from his car ashtray, while another Knockemstiffer steals drugs intended for his girlfriend's stroke-victim father. Drugs of choice include marijuana, meth, mescaline, hashish, angel dust and OxyContin. And the use of drugs in Knockemstiff was not only prolific, it was also creative. While sharing the suggestion that you not try this at home, who knew that Seconal could be inventively internalized in suppository form?

17 ~ KICK IN DE KÖK, ESTONIA ~ Talk about having your bell rung, this one hurts the guys in our audience more than any other in the book. On the subject of pain, please allow us to share this additional fun fact. Cannon balls dating back to 1577 are still embedded in the outer walls of the Kick In de Kök tower. For what it's worth, the etymology of the quirky name comes from the German language, a result of the fact that modern-day Estonia, was part of the German-speaking Prussian Empire when the name was established. The general German meaning of the phrase "Kick In de Kök" translates to "lookout tower."

16 ~ TAYLOR'S MISTAKE, NEW ZEALAND ~ This quaint, coastal New Zealand town inevitably poses the question of, "Who is this Taylor dude and what was his mistake?" The answer to that question actually takes on an air of Twilight Zone eeriness. Within a span of just a dozen years in the mid-19th century there were three different maritime mishaps, all of which involved a man named Taylor! How weird is that? Those three stories are too much to include in our countdown here, but we will provide a nutshell summary of what people said they liked most about this entry. In addition to the Taylor mistakes, there's also the story of the insurance fraud involving a faked death, a severed and stolen human arm, and a humiliating call-to-justice conclusion.

15 ~ TWATT, SCOTLAND ~ If Scotland wasn't already your favorite country, it will be soon. Believe it or not, the Scots have two Twatts. Yep, there are only two geographic locations on the planet called "Twatt" and they're both in Scotland. "Here Kitty, Kitty," was a line we couldn't resist using. If you hit the internet looking for the Top 10 Things to do in either Twatt, our extensive research reveals that #1 on the list is stand next to the road sign with an arrow pointing your way. The Twatt in the Shetland Islands is the bigger one, sometimes preferable, as it has a few hundred inhabitants. If you'd prefer a smaller, tighter Twatt community, head for the Orkney Islands. Their population comes in at under a hundred. Fully analyzing the etymology angle, we should go on to acknowledge that, in addition to being a euphemism for vagina, "twat" is also used in English to mean a weak or contemptible individual. So with that in mind, next time you find yourself vacationing in the Scotish Isles, don't pose by the Twatt sign unless your level of self-confidence sufficiently supports the pose. People could take this picture two ways.

14 ~ EGGS AND BACON BAY, TASMANIA ~ It was a beautiful sunny-side-up morning in Eggs and Bacon Bay, Tasmania, when suddenly the mood was pooh-poohed by those prissy PETA people pandering political correctness, or the purported lack thereof, on the part of the residents of Eggs and Bacon Bay. PETA was proffering the proposal that E&BB change its name to a more animal-friendly "Apple and Cherry Bay." Prior to filing their petition for the change in 2016, PETA Australia's associate director of campaigns, Ashley Fruno, had submitted a letter to Mayor Peter Coad of Eggs and Bacon Bay informing him that Tasmania had the highest level of lap band surgery in all of Australia, and to help halt that hideous health statistic, Fruno suggested that residents abstain from cholesterol and fat-laden bacon and eggs. It's a great story about how PETA ends up with egg on its face and here's our takeaway. If you ever consider having lap band surgery, just remember, PETA is watching.

13 ~ FUCKING, AUSTRIA~ Sure it's a tough name to live with, but since 1994 the town has held three votes regarding a name replacement, and not a fucking thing has changed. One conceptual thread that runs through this book is this scenario where centuries ago people in a foreign country gave their town a name that had a funky meaning in English but had no connection whatsoever to any meaning in the native language. In the 9th century A.D. when a community of Austrians named their town Fucking, who knew? But a millennium later with the internet linking a global community, everyone knows. So why keep the name? The actual reasons are financial which we explain in the book, but here's our favorite one. Fucking resident Helga Fritzenhopper has one of the "Welcome to Fucking" signs in her yard. When asked if she voted for the name change, her answer was, "Fuck No. I haven't had sex for the past 25 years since my husband Adolph died. With that Fucking sign in my yard, I get to see live sex half a dozen times a year. That's a pretty nice number because it actually about equals what I was getting when Adolph was alive, and now I don't even have to wash the sheets."

12 ~ HELL, MICHIGAN ~ As we've taken you on our tour of fanciful place names, this is one of the few that has taken its quirky name, run with it, and managed to turn itself into a full-fledged tourist attraction. Hell is located in the southeastern part of the state, 15 miles northwest of Ann Arbor, which is the home of the University of Michigan. And there is definitely kind of a college-town vibe burning in Hell. The town has implemented a variety of kitschy activities and unusual gifts and knickknacks making use of the town's name. The establishment that is the base of operations for many of the activities is *Screams Souvenirs from Hell*. At *Screams* it is possible to make arrangements to get married, become Mayor for the day, or literally become the legal owner of your own little piece of Hell. What the devil more could you ask for? Hell, Michigan is a very festive creative place where a lot of thought has gone into numerous clever ways to play upon the satanic title of the town. Devilish fun has begun! So, if the whole shebang sounds like a shindig sure to satisfy, you can get all fired up and go to Hell!

11 ~ JIM THORPE, PENNSYLVANIA ~ Of all the locations we have ever visited, here is our most uniquely bizarre story regarding the naming of a place. Please join us in a somewhat creepy convoy to the Keystone State. Located deep in the heart of Pennsylvania is the picturesque town of Jim Thorpe. As one might suspect the town is named after the famous athlete, but the circumstances of how the town came to bear Jim Thorpe's name bizarrely border on the morbidly macabre. The town was originally named Mauch Chunk and was hoping to switch to something a little less repulsive when Jim Thorpe's death in 1953 sparked a twisted turn. The town talked Thorpe's widow, who was not the mother of any of his eight children, into selling his corpse in order to erect a shrine facilitating the renaming of this Pennsylvania town. So, let it be known, Jim Thorpe never set foot in Jim Thorpe.

10 ~ DILDO, CANADA ~ The name of this town has frequently become a source of celebrity and in the 20th century there were several campaigns to change the name, though all failed. Probably a good thing; history should always trump hysteria. It was through the magic of television that Jimmy Kimmel provided Dildo with its proverbial 15 minutes of fame just within the past few years. Actually it turned into more like a week of fame and the full story is in the book. It was in August of 2019 that *Jimmy Kimmel Live!* made Dildo the focus of attention over a number of shows. As part of the series, he was made honorary mayor of Dildo and Kimmel declared Hollywood to be Dildo's sister city. In addition to this grandiose gesture, he also gifted the community with a giant "DILDO" sign (in the style of the classic "HOLLYWOOD" sign) which sits on the hillside overlooking the Canadian community. At this point the conservatives in the community who had previously lobbied for a name change had to be conquered. The only thing worse than having a huge Dildo sign looming large over your hamlet's horizon would be the dire situation of having no current explanation of what it's there for.

9 ~ BATMAN, TURKEY ~ Batman is a city of about 350,000 located in southeast Turkey, within the province of Batman. For the record there's also a Batman River. Until the 1950's it was a small town of about 3,000. Then oil was discovered and all hell broke loose in Batman. As Robin, the Boy Wonder, might have said, "Holy 10,000% population increase, Batman!" This town in Turkey that bears his name has taken on a somewhat bizarre relationship with the Dark Knight. In the book we tell you about how they've done all of the following.

- Sued Warner Bros. over the movies.
- Blamed Batman for an increased teen suicide rate.
- Attempted to gerrymander its boundary to the shape of the Bat-Signal.

This reconfiguring of the map has taken on some unique implications in this ethnically tense area where the Turks and the Kurds don't agree on much, but the one cause they could coalesce upon was a joint initiative to gerrymander the map and have the province boundaries reconfigured into the shape of the Bat-Signal. In fairness to its neighbors, a petition was initiated that calls for Batman to acquire and concede equal amounts of land in order to achieve the reconfiguration. Google "Batman Turkey Petition" and you can get caught up on the whole story.

8 ~ RABBIT HASH, KENTUCKY ~ Located in the northernmost county in Kentucky, Rabbit Hash is a small town with a population of 315. While it may be small in size, it's large in storylines. In addition to its unusual name, Rabbit Hash has one of the country's most historic general stores and since 1998, the town has elected a dog to the office of mayor. After a series of male mayors, a border collie named Lucy Lou was elected as the first female mayor of Rabbit Hash in 2008. Her prominence probably pinnacled on September 7, 2015, when her office announced that she was considering a run for the presidency of the United States. After careful consideration, Lucy determined that the office was beneath her and decided to retire from politics altogether. One accolade Lucy Lou could take to the grave with her… she certainly lived up to the promise she campaigned upon when she declared herself, "The Bitch you can count on." Lucy Lou was succeeded by the current mayor, a pit bull named Brynneth Pawltro, or "Brynn" as her friends call her. How did the town get its name? According to popular legend, a flood in the 1840's drove hundreds of rabbits from the riverbank, and right into the stew pots of hungry settlers. It was rabbit hash all around.

7 ~ RAGGED ASS ROAD, CANADA ~ The best things in life are worth fighting for, right? While the success wasn't achieved without controversy, by the time the community of Yellowknife in the Northwest Territories of Canada officially held its festivities for the 50th Anniversary of Ragged Ass Road in 2020, the street name to which some had originally objected had become a source of community pride. Ragged Ass Road has put Yellowknife on the map and made it the source of multiple pop culture references. As is often the case with great stories in the Northwest Territories, it all started with a bunch of drunken gold prospectors. The group was led by a dude named Lou Rocher and while drinking their blues away after a difficult prospecting season had yielded little income, Rocher joked that since they were all "ragged ass broke," they might as well make that the name of the street. The gag caught on and Ragged Ass Road became the unofficial name. The men put up a sign that night. Lou Rocher died in May 2013 and was remembered around Yellowknife most prominently for giving Ragged Ass Road its name. Despite that, his family noted, at that time the city still had not installed official street signs with the name. In 2015 official Ragged Ass Road signs were erected at both ends of the road. Sometimes you have to die to get your due.

6 ~ SANTA CLAUS, ARIZONA ~ You'll find no shortage of ghost towns along Route 66, but one of the strangest by far has to be the abandoned town of Santa Claus, Arizona. The Mojave Desert, with its blisteringly hot summer sun, Joshua trees and bizarre rock formations, would not generally be the place one would choose to honor a man whose traditional home is the North Pole. Yet standing in the desert are the ghostly remnants of Santa Claus, Arizona. The rise and fall of the town is a tale that truly tugs at your heartstrings. It sprung literally out of nowhere when a patch of barren desert was developed into a Christmas-themed park complete with a restaurant, hotel and a variety of kitschy shops and attractions. From its inception through the 1960's Santa Claus thrived on what was America's iconic east-west thoroughfare, Route 66, a bustling, year-round holiday-themed stop for road-tripping motorists. But when newer interstates essentially replaced Route 66, the glory days of Santa Claus were equally doomed. Sadly, and ironically, the rattlesnakes now outnumber the reindeer in the ramshackle ruins remaining here.

5 ~ CHICKEN, ALASKA ~ In our ongoing quest to tell the stories behind the most uniquely named places on the planet, rarely did we laugh as hard as we did when we visited the website for Chicken, Alaska. It is an enigmatic place with more stories in one town than there are eggs in a hen house. There are so many storylines, it's almost hard to know where to start. There's also a nice variety of Chicken merchandise available including t-shirts, baseball caps, and beer koozies. Their #1 seller is what they refer to as their "famous and classy" t-shirt which shows a chicken breaking out of an egg with the caption "I got laid in Chicken." We're sure that's a goal shared by many but realized by few. The website includes an option on buying the whole downtown complex of Chicken along with some titillating tidbits on what is included in the offer and what is not. For example, in the saloon the deal is "underwear stapled to the ceiling included ~ panty cannon is negotiable." For us, we're thinking the inclusion of the panty cannon would be pretty much a make-or-break component of the deal. So we spoke to Sue Wiren the owner and got her personal explanation. Sue said, "The panty cannon is fired by black powder, and wadding partly comprised of panties. We also use a fuse so you can run like hell, once the fuse is lit. It is blown off in the parking lot and is not done on demand. It is the bartender's prerogative and is done for the pure fun and joy."

4 - KIESTER, MINNESOTA - Kiester's 15 minutes of fame came when the pharmaceutical company Pfizer offered the town big bucks if they would roll out their red carpet and take advantage of their aptly named town to host a commercial for their Preparation H hemorrhoid medication. After many years of being the butt of many jokes, the 501 kiesters in Kiester decided it was time to take Pfizer up on their offer and laugh their asses off all the way to the bank. And it turned out to be one kick-ass commercial. You absolutely will not believe what they managed to shove into one 15-second spot. It starts out with one smokin' hot chick posed at the "Welcome to Kiester" sign, her ass firmly planted on a bicycle seat. The hot chick's opening line of the commercial is, "You wouldn't believe what's in this Kiester." In the following 15 seconds the girl verbally salutes Kiester's Farmer's Market, Marching Band, and Fire Department. If you can take your eyes off her ass long enough to notice, the background features the Kiester Market, school, theatre and if by this point you're looking for something to blow your snow, Kiester Implement lies right ahead.

3 - EIGHTY EIGHT, KENTUCKY - There are three dates that will always stand out as being the red-letter days in the history of Eighty Eight, Kentucky. Those dates are November 2, 1948, August 8, 1988, and August 8, 2008. Here's why these days are special. The final tally in the 1948 election in the town of Eighty Eight was Truman 88, Dewey 88. Honest to God! That trifecta earned the town its first real claim to fame. The 88 to 88 in Eighty Eight enshrined the town in *Ripley's Believe It Or Not* thus immortalizing Eighty Eight forever. The other two days had to do with the name of the town and the appeal of getting that name on the postmark of letters mailed on significant dates. The 1988 date was a total blowout including a huge parade and live network TV coverage with a torrent of people wanting to be a part of 8/8/88 in the town of Eighty Eight. Two decades later the whole shebang was repeated on 08/08/08. So what's up next for the town? Mark your calendars for August 8, 2088 when it once again will be 8/8/88 in Eighty Eight. We hope to see you there.

2 ~ LEG-IN-BOOT, CANADA ~ Here's a name certain to raise some eyebrows. Or give people cause to seek out their marching orders, half of them anyway. Here's the scoop… In 1887 a full half of a human leg washed up on the shores of nearby False Creek, still wearing its boot. Baffled by the severed extremity, the constables seemingly decided that rather than pounding the pavement trying to identify its owner, they would simply spear the leg on a spike and leave it outside the precinct office in case the owner came by looking for it. Passersby were too stunned to look and too stunned to leave. Perhaps not surprisingly, the lost leg went unclaimed and after two weeks was assumedly thrown out or simply given to a stray dog in keeping with the apparent police disinterest in expending any man hours on the case. Sometimes an 800-pound gorilla is really an 800-pound gorilla.

1 ~ SATAN'S KINGDOM, CONNECTICUT ~ The name originally stemmed from the fact that the area was plagued by rocky, unfertile soil, which made it unconducive for farming, therefore it was not a place a lot of people wanted to go. But that's not what drove this story to #1 in the voting we received. There are towns named Satan's Kingdom in both the neighboring states of Vermont and Massachusetts. So what makes this Kingdom so special? It's the unique supplementary material associated with the storyline. A common theme we've seen with towns bearing unique names is that by their very uniqueness, the signs often become targets for theft. Different towns in our book took different approaches to battling this problem. These approaches varied from bigger screws to GPS attachments to two-ton signs, but the greatest idea of all was the stroke of genius that hit Satan's Kingdom. At this point we will defer to one of our respondents who rated the stories in our book. She wrote, "You guys absolutely killed it on this one, pun intended, and I can give you a very specific reason why. I thought the brilliance of the Satan's Kingdom sign strategy could never be equaled until I saw how funny the story was that you came up with to culminate the saga. It was the ultimate one-two-punch. Well done."

ADDENDUM #2 ~ THE POETRY

This one's for the poetry lovers in our audience. Here we have collected all of the poems we wrote for this book. If you recall from way back in the beginning we started off with a sonnet in our prologue replicating a motif sometimes used by Shakespeare. A sonnet is a 14-line poem with a rhyme scheme of abab, cdcd, efef, gg. Everything else is a limerick following back on the classic rhyme scheme of aabba.

PROLOGUE

We pose the question here, "What's in a name?
We'll span the world to write this travelogue
In Rabbit Hash the mayor's claim to fame
Comes from the fact the seat's held by a dog

Alaska's Chicken has our favorite tricks
The panty cannon really is a blast
That Santa Claus adorned Route 66
But changing times assured it wouldn't last

Hell, Michigan where people come to pray
And folks do like to have their weddings there
The Leg-In-Boot town finds a limb and they
Impale it on a spike right in the square

With Weed and papers we will get Skyhigh
We'll Knockemstiff in Stoner, that's no lie

SONNETS

CHAPTER 1 ~ STORYLINE SAMPLER

No plumbing, don't be panic-stricken
But your pace to the outhouse might quicken
You're pissed off and swearing
But at least you're bearing
Gifts saying, "I got laid in Chicken!"

It washed up on the shore over there
Just one leg in a boot solitaire
What the hell do we do?
We just feel inclined to
Stick the leg on a stake in the square

On the rooftop sometimes Santa pauses
Naming places with holiday causes
Our one "Christmas" extols
There are two "North Poles"
And then alas three "Santa Clauses"

CHAPTER 2 ~ FOOD FOR THOUGHT

We like Egg-Bacon Bay to defeat a
Name changing vote to complete a
Move to just place
The egg on the face
Of those tree-hugging vegans at PETA

In 'Bama they love fun and games
Some places down there have great names
But their Bottle of Nehi
That stood sixty feet high
Went up in a blaze of orange flames

CHAPTER 3 ~ DRINKS ARE ON US

Underwater you see the town's crossing
Whiskeytown had us turning and tossing
Just try to rhyme Toadsuck
Nightmares ... what the fuck!
Let's go get high at Beer Bottle Crossing

CHAPTER 4 ~ HIGH TIMES

In Weed she'll score pot from a donor
In Zigzag some papers they'll loan her
While tokin' she'll fly for
She'll soon be Skyhigh for
That Bong-a-Thon fired up in Stoner

CHAPTER 5 ~ HOW DO YOU LIKE THOSE MELONS?

Sugar Tit is a name that's unique
The Office Girls flaunt their mystique
Titicaca just will
Adore Titty Hill
Antarctica has Nipple Peak

Roman conquest was a shitty pill
For England to swallow, but 'twill
Inspire the Brits
To show us their tits
And go rename their town Titty Hill

CHAPTER 6 ~ COCK-A-DOODLE-DOO

A Kick in the Cock is rejection
A Condom provides some protection
Look for your next bang
And get a Wet Wang
Resulting in your New Erection

CHAPTER 7 ~ WHAT'S UP PUSSYCAT?

Beaverlick, it does have a mystique
Those Muff divers love Pussy Creek
Hats off to the Scots
Cause they have two Twatts
Pussy, France we salute tongue-in-cheek

CHAPTER 8 - THE JOY OF SEX

There once was a man from Nantucket
Whose Orgy in Dildo, he ducked it
Come By Chance, no not he
Opted out for plan B
Went to Thailand and visited Phuket

Humptulips does sound rather sick
We do much prefer Beaverlick
Before our Wet Wang
We'll watch the Big Bang
Episode that we love "Pennycomequick"

Horneytown's found in North Carolina
France's Orgy was in Indochina
In Sexmoan they're sucking
While Austria's Fucking
Russia changes a name to Vagina

CHAPTER 9 - WORD PLAY

In Key West we could try vermouth
Eye for an eye and a tooth for a tooth
Or we could try sex
In the streets of Zzyzx
Then choose Consequences or Truth

CHAPTER 10 - EXCLAMATIONS! – QUESTIONS? – COMMANDS.

Why or Why Not, just give me a sec
Pity Me, albatross 'round my neck
Shout "Eek," cry "Good Grief!"
Where to find some relief?
Saint-Louis-Du-Ha!-Ha!, Quebec

CHAPTER 11 ~ IT'S A NUMBERS GAME

The 88 cents sealed the fate
Established forever the date
There'd be no debate
The ratings were great
On 8/8/88, Eighty Eight

When the meeting was all said and done
Time does fly when you're just having rum
Or was it the wine?
When they did see the sign
Blueberry became Wonowon

CHAPTER 12 ~ NOT FOR NOTHING

Let's put somebody's nose out of joint
Kings of nothingness we will anoint
There's no prizes to claim
No Place or No Name
Going Nowhere but to Point No Point

CHAPTER 13 ~ DON'T BE SO NEGATIVE

Useless Loop's at the end of its rope
Misery Bay's got a slippery slope
Strange but it's true
There's Peculiar, Mizzou
Worst of all we still have Little Hope

CHAPTER 14 ~ FROM MEDIOCRE TO BORING

Dull, Boring and Bland were all hurtin'
For tourism to raise the curtain
What the hell could we say
Were they Lost or Okay?
Of the answer we feel quite Uncertain

CHAPTER 15 ~ OUR BODY OF WORK

It washed up on the shore over there
Just one leg in a boot solitaire
What the hell do we do?
We just feel inclined to
Stick the leg on a stake in the square

See the girl on the bike and at least your
Certainly pleased she's surceased her
Attempts to play coy then
She'll be your sex toy when
She wants you to check out her Kiester

Flight attendant with his balls of brass
Said, "Take off that shirt, it's so crass"
But times they would change
And rules rearrange
Now they all love the road Ragged Ass

CHAPTER 16 ~ PAIN IN THE ASS

See the girl on the bike and at least your
Certainly pleased she's surceased her
Attempts to play coy then
She'll be your sex toy when
She wants you to check out her Kiester

Flight attendant with his balls of brass
Said, "Take off that shirt, it's so crass"
But times they would change
And rules rearrange
Now they all love the road Ragged Ass

CHAPTER 17 ~ OOH, THAT'S GROSS

The Boogerhole murders chagrined
The Shitterton sign stealers sinned
We can't Poo Poo Pee Pee
So then I just guess we
Leave Middelfart for Brokenwind

CHAPTER 18 ~ BATMAN, THE DARK KNIGHT

Batman, Turkey's a place where they lied
Sued Warners but they were denied
Stuck to their claim for
Pinning the blame for
Their wave of increased suicide

CHAPTER 19 ~ A ZOOTOPIAN EXPERIENCE

The Rabbit Hash dog / pony show
Dogs get their ducks all in a row
The town loved Lucy Lou
Who passed the baton to
A mayor who's named Brynneth Pawltro

No plumbing, don't be panic-stricken
But your pace to the outhouse might quicken
You're pissed off and swearing
But at least you're bearing
Gifts saying, "I got laid in Chicken!"

More animal stories we've planned
Our Chicken piece turned out just grand
Mousie sounds fun
Big Beaver could run
A town that is called Bird-in-Hand

CHAPTER 20 ~ JUSTIFYING THE JIM THORPE THEFT

Pennsylvania, sometimes the mind warps
Things can change at the drop of a corpse
Mauch Chunk go away
We've a new name to say
That's because the dead corpse was Jim Thorpe's

CHAPTER 21 ~ HOME FOR THE HOLIDAYS

On the rooftop sometimes Santa pauses
Naming places with holiday causes
Our one "Christmas" extols
There are two "North Poles"
And then alas three "Santa Clauses"

The restaurant had cakes, shakes and steaks
Festive holiday scenes with snow flakes
But when Route 66
No longer had kicks
The reindeer gave way to the snakes

CHAPTER 22 ~ THE WILD WILD WEST

We cross our hearts and hope to die
The O.K. Corral was a lie
And you can't tip your hat
To the bad Shootout at
The Photo Shop of C.S. Fly

CHAPTER 23 ~ YOU'RE KILLING US

This chapter comes hell or high water
Delaware's got a beach that's called Slaughter
We'll hit Deadhorse too
And chart our course to
Dead Horse Bay where we won't drink the water

With Calamity Jane by his side
It was Deadwood where Wild Bill died
We'll visit Fresh Kills
And then Kill Devil Hills
Where the Wright brothers turned glide to flied

CHAPTER 24 ~ GO TO HELL

Satan's Kingdoms' signs they all said "Satan's"
With sign theft they did lose their patience
Sober plan by the owners
To perplex the stoners
Let's misspell the sign to say "Statan's"

In Michigan's Hell you can say
I own land and it's my wedding day
And just to convey that
You will be the fat cat
You're Mayor of Hell for the day

ABOUT THE AUTHORS

We have a rather unique back story, most of which is set in upstate New York. We met on the first day of high school, brought together by the merger of two neighboring school districts. We ended up dating for all four years of high school, then went to different colleges and, as fate would have it, we ended up not seeing each other again for literally 40 years.

Tim's mom passed away a few years ago and Deb heard about it through the grapevine in Virginia Beach where she was teaching. She sent him a sympathy card, he wrote back, one thing led to another and Tim ended up coming down to Virginia Beach at the end of that school year to pick Deb up and bring her back home to New York.

The thing Deb remembers most from that courtship period when she was in Virginia, but longing to be back in New York, was that every day at school when she went to her mailbox, there was an envelope from Tim. And each one contained an original letter Deb had written to him 40 years ago. He had saved every one. His go-to line regarding that part of the story is to say, "Yeah, it took me a long time to play those cards!" Sometimes the best things in life are worth waiting for.

We got engaged on Deb's mother's birthday (December 4) and we got married on Tim's mother's birthday (June 12). Because we both have Native American ancestry, we had the ceremony performed at the Ganondagan Historic Site by the Native American leader there, as well as a former student of Tim's.

So how did we get into this writing gig? Well, as fate would have it, we happen to live right next door to the newspaper office in our town. After hearing some of our stories, the publisher of the paper, Chris Carosa, suggested we write about our background and share it with the community. So we started by telling the personal story of our relationship and we haven't stopped writing since. Currently our weekly feature comprises the entire back page of the *Mendon-Honeoye Falls-Lima Sentinel* and we have now upped our production to include two more columns within the paper. Contributing to the community is a passion of ours.

We write about an eclectic variety of topics including entertainment, sports, travel, history and human interest. Chris Carosa, who we mentioned above, had been encouraging us to write a book since we first began writing for the paper. That first book came to fruition in 2019 with the publication of *The Beatles, The Bible & Manson: Reflecting Back with 50 Years of Perspective* in the summer of 2019. We followed up in 2020 with *Tit For Tat Exchanges ~ Tim & Deb's Greatest Hits* which we described in the "Acknowledgements" component in the beginning of this book. And at this point we hope you've just finished *What's in a Name?* and have enjoyed it so much you'll be interested in checking out the rest of our work.

www.ingramcontent.com/pod-product-compliance
Lightning Source LLC
Chambersburg PA
CBHW061306110426
42742CB00012BA/2079